A

DANCE

with

JANE AUSTEN

A DANCE *with* JANE AUSTEN

How a Novelist and Her Characters Went to the Ball

Susannah Fullerton

F

FRANCES LINCOLN LIMITED
PUBLISHERS

To Amanda Jones,
with love and thanks for friendship, book talk,
and the world's most generous loans of books.

Frances Lincoln Limited
www.franceslincoln.com

A Dance with Jane Austen
Copyright © Frances Lincoln Limited 2012
Text copyright © Susannah Fullerton 2012
Illustrations copyright as on page 158
First Frances Lincoln edition 2012

A catalogue record for this book is available from the British Library.

9-780-7112-3245-7

Printed and bound in China

1 2 3 4 5 6 7 8 9

Contents

A Modern Belle going to the Rooms at Bath.

Pub Jan.r 13.th 1796. by
H. Humphrey, New Bond Street

Foreword

Some modern readers of Jane Austen's novels are apt to dismiss them out of hand as being rather dull and repetitive – 'There's always a dance scene in them, every one!' – and leave their criticism at that. Such readers are of course accurate in stating this fact even though wrong in their interpretation of it. There are indeed dance scenes in each of the novels, because in Regency times the dance floor was the best place upon which to meet one's future husband or wife. Assembly balls in a country town would draw together young people from an approximately twenty-mile radius who might not otherwise have come into contact with each other, since a twenty-mile journey would have taken about four hours' travelling time and so was not to be lightly undertaken.

In this book Susannah Fullerton has analysed all the aspects of dances and dancing as personally experienced by Jane Austen and mentioned by her in her letters to her sister Cassandra; and has studied all mentions of dances in the novels to show how they advance the plot as well as adding to the skilful betrayal of the nature and motives of some of the characters in the tale. No one who has read Susannah's in-depth analysis could possibly ever think again that Jane Austen's dance scenes are either dull or repetitive; but will be left feeling regretful that there are no more aspects left to be discussed.

DEIRDRE LE FAYE

Introduction

'May I have the pleasure of this dance?'

When a gentleman asked Jane Austen that question, she was delighted to stand up with him. Jane Austen loved to dance. 'There were twenty dances & I danced them all, & without any fatigue', she recorded happily in a letter. Her correspondence is full of references to balls, who were her partners, and which couples flirted the most while they danced. Throughout her life she attended informal dances at the homes of neighbours, grander events in the houses of the local gentry, and dances at home with relations and friends. This book tells the story of her dancing life and how much she enjoyed it.

With such a love of elegantly moving to music, how could Jane Austen possibly leave dancing out of her novels? When too young to attend balls herself, she could still create fictional ones in her juvenilia. When an adult, she depicted a dance in every one of her six novels; some, such as *Pride and Prejudice*, contain several. Her unfinished work *The Watsons* provides her most detailed description of a ball to be found in her fiction.

Jane Austen wrote for her contemporaries, who would all have been very familiar with the many different aspects of a ball. As modern readers, we have lost much of that knowledge. The Bennet girls dance at an assembly ball – but what was an assembly ball and who was permitted to attend one? How were the Bennets expected to dress for the occasion? What would they have eaten for supper at the end of the evening? When men asked them to join a set, who provided the music? And what sorts of dances did Elizabeth and Jane need to know? Woe betide any Lydia Bennet who broke the rules of etiquette at a dance – but what were the rules? This book describes the dances, the facilities, the rules and customs of the ballrooms of Jane Austen's era and fiction.

Shakespeare's Romeo and Juliet fell in love at a ball. From *Romeo and Juliet* to *Harry Potter*, balls have been recognized as a vital arena for courtship. Jane Austen fell in love with Tom Lefroy as they danced together and their romance was conducted almost entirely at balls. In her fiction she depicts lovers, would-be lovers, disappointed lovers and those-who-are-lovers-but-don't-yet-realize-it, all dancing in the ballrooms of southern England. Where would the courtship of Elizabeth and Mr Darcy be without the Meryton assembly and the Netherfield ball? Dance plays such an integral role as hero and heroine of *Pride and Prejudice* fall in love. The same can be said for another couple in that novel: Jane and Mr Bingley also move from being dance partners to marriage partners. Catherine Morland is smitten by Henry Tilney at a Bath ball, Marianne and Willoughby of *Sense and Sensibility* have eyes only for each other when they dance at Barton Park, Emma first begins to see Mr Knightley as a possible lover at the Crown Inn ball, and for Fanny Price, the highlight of the Mansfield ball is when she dances with Edmund. Among Jane Austen's heroines, only Elinor Dashwood and Anne Elliot are given no opportunity to dance with the men they love.

LUN

This book shows how Jane Austen's fictional courtships begin and progress on the dance floor.

But there was no guarantee of finding true love at a ball. Jane Austen knew the horrors of a bad partner – she tried hard to avoid certain men at dances because they had two left feet. Her heroines suffer the same problems. Catherine is desperate to escape John Thorpe, while Elizabeth is almost tortured by bumbling Mr Collins. Other dance partners in the novels are simply mismatched – Henry Crawford with Fanny Price, Louisa Musgrove with Captain Wentworth, and Harriet Smith with Mr Knightley. 'To be fond of dancing' was not invariably 'a certain step towards falling in love'; or at least, towards falling in love with the right person.

This book also examines the social milieu of the dance. Balls were one of the few activities that Regency men and women could enjoy together. Sir John Middleton has his hunting and other sports, his wife has children and domestic pursuits to keep her busy – but a ball brings husband and wife together. And it brings their neighbours and friends too, all joining in a communal activity, socializing, and forming attractive patterns with other dancers to be admired by any spectators. As dancers, they all have certain obligations. Mr Darcy, dramatically entering for the first time both *Pride and Prejudice* and the Meryton assem-

UDDING

bly room, appears 'above his company' and refuses to invite local girls to dance. Mr Elton rudely shows up Harriet Smith by strutting before her instead of leading her into the set and John Thorpe is late to claim Catherine for their dance, which embarrasses her. Jane Austen always had a sharp eye for incorrect behaviour when she attended balls, and she accurately portrayed such social blunders or improprieties in her novels. Elizabeth I insisted all her courtiers learn to dance, and excel at the art, because she believed dance developed not only well-regulated body movements but a well-regulated mind as well. This view had not changed by Jane Austen's day, and conduct book authors were still stressing the importance of dance as a reflection of the mind and personality. One arbiter of manners, Lord Chesterfield, thought dancing a ridiculous activity, yet he still advised his son Philip to become proficient. Look at how much can be determined about Mr Collins solely from his behaviour at a ball. Or of Mr Bingley, or John Thorpe.

Mrs Bennet takes her daughters to balls, but her own dancing days are over. Fortunately for her, there was always plenty going on at the edges of a ballroom – the chaperones gossiping by the fire, card parties in a side room, alcoholic refreshment for those who (like Jane Austen in middle age) were happy to sit and watch, with a glass of wine at hand. When the musicians needed a break, there was musical entertainment (and Mary Bennet loves such opportunities to display) or there were the men who, eager to gaze on the Georgian equivalent of eye-candy, strutted the room, ogling the local talent (Lord Osborne in *The Watsons* is one such example). Miss Bates chatters nonstop at balls, General Tilney does his social networking there, Mrs Norris disrupts and irritates, but what did a master of ceremonies do? What were the duties of those chaperones and bystanders; why were so many young ladies without partners; what was on the menu in the supper room? Jane Austen never wasted a word in her novels – whenever she provides detail of a ball, readers can be sure it is there for a purpose, an important part of characterization or plot. Dancing is an ancient human activity – rock paintings depict dancers in 3300 BC. It has always been a vital part of human culture – for celebration, ritual, courtship, and for telling stories. Jane Austen recognized its importance.

Jane Austen loved to put on her satin slippers with shoe-roses, her white gloves and muslin gown, and go off for an evening of fun at the Basingstoke assemblies. The Bennet girls share their creator's delight and set out joyfully to dance, and of course to meet future husbands. Why not do Elizabeth and Jane the honour of joining them, as they dance their way through this book? Follow Jane Austen's heroines, as they learn their steps, dress in readiness, find transport to convey them to a ball, choose between public and private balls, worry over a shortage of men, prefer a cotillion to a quadrille, talk and flirt with their partners, sustain themselves with supper, fall in love, and then go home to talk it all over at the end.

And now, 'On with the dance . . . '

The Figures shew the positions of the Learner, and the Feet that of a finish'd Dancer.

Learning to dance

'We . . . had all the masters that were necessary.'
PRIDE AND PREJUDICE

According to Mr Darcy, 'every savage can dance', but Mr Darcy is wrong. A savage would actually have struggled badly and his gyrations would have been watched with horror at any of the three balls that take place in *Pride and Prejudice* – the Meryton assembly, the informal dance at Sir William Lucas's and the ball at Netherfield.

Mr Collins is as close as we get to a savage in that novel, for he has not been properly taught to dance, so embarrasses himself and those who come near him. Having him as her partner is a miserable experience for Elizabeth Bennet: 'they were dances of mortification. Mr Collins, awkward and solemn, apologising instead of attending, and often moving wrong without being aware of it' is a torment to her. 'The moment of her release from him was exstacy.'

Fortunately most people attending balls were better instructed than Mr Collins. Learning to dance was an important accomplishment for ladies and gentlemen, so was included in any genteel or semi-genteel education. Fashionable schools, such as those attended by the daughters of Mrs Jennings, stressed that dancing was 'one of the most genteel and polite Accomplishments which a young Lady can possess' and Miss Bingley is quick to include it in her list of essential accomplishments for an elegant female. Dance instruction was thought to teach graceful deportment, to polish manners, and to provide healthy exercise. When Elizabeth tells Lady Catherine de Bourgh that she and her sisters 'had all the masters that were necessary', it can be safely assumed that one would have come to Longbourn. It is also safe to assume that he would

have been the only visiting instructor to earn the full attention of Lydia Bennet, who, as foolish as she was, knew that dancing was one thing she had to do properly.

The steps of a country dance were relatively simple and there were not many of them. But more than country dancing was taught – a pupil must acquire elegant movements of the arms, the correct general carriage ('should be elevated and light; the chest thrown out, the head easily erect, but flexible to move with every turn of the figure; and the limbs should be all braced with the spirit of motion'), and there was bowing and curtseying, and the etiquette of the ballroom to learn as well. The minuet, although not danced so often by Jane Austen's day, was always taught to young people because its formal movements were seen as a good instructional groundwork. Once the minuet was mastered, the teacher could move on to demonstrating other steps.

The dancing master visiting Longbourn could well have been shared by other families – perhaps the Lucas girls joined in the lessons? Such arrangements made it more social and enjoyable for those participating and increased the number of possible partners and 'couples' in the lesson, but also lessened the expense for one family. Often great houses in a neighbourhood offered local young people shared dance classes. The Duchess of Devonshire, renowned socialite and tastemaker, organized morning classes in her home, so that young ladies living near Chatsworth could master their dance steps together. Children's balls were relatively common throughout the Georgian age; they provided a relaxed opportunity for young people to show off what they had learned and

get used to the formalities of the ballroom.

But when no ball especially for children was offered, young people were taken to adult balls. Charles Blake of *The Watsons*, 'a fine boy of ten years old', is brought to the assembly ball by his mother because he is 'uncommonly fond of dancing'. He has had to learn the right etiquette, has asked his partner a week in advance to secure her for 'the two first dances', and he has to learn to hide his great disappointment when his partner rudely lets him down: 'though he contrived to utter with an effort of boyish bravery "Oh! I do not mind it" – it was very evident by the unceasing agitation of his features that he minded it as much as ever'. When Emma then says she would be happy to be his partner, Charles is given his opportunity. Although concentrating very hard on his steps, he is also mindful of his other duties as a partner – making conversation, keeping on his gloves and thanking Emma properly when their dance is over. The scene provides a charming picture of a boy trying very hard to appear sophisticated in this adult setting, yet unable to stop his boyish enthusiasms breaking through every now and then. Although he is the only child Jane Austen mentions in a ballroom, there must have been many Charles Blakes in England learning vital lessons about dance steps, the rules and regulations, and good manners, which would turn them into accomplished partners as adults.

In *Mansfield Park* the Price family cannot afford a dancing master so the children have to teach themselves. William reminds his sister of how they used to 'jump about together many a time . . . when the hand-organ was in the street', but this lack of formal instruction leaves Fanny rather uncertain so she assiduously practises her steps in the drawing room before the Mansfield ball begins.

Fanny is aware that Mary Crawford has learned to dance in London, and there dance classes were more sophisticated. A newspaper of 1784 advertised instruction in 'the Minuet, Minuet de la Cour, Cotillons' and offered regular opportunities for practice. Many young women in London wanted to learn from professional dancers of the Opera House as this made them appear more sophisticated (lessons that would appeal to Miss Bingley perhaps?) but Thomas Wilson disapproved and felt such teachers distorted the graceful, easy steps of the country dance into 'extravagant theatrical imitations'. Nor was it only ladies who worried about being up-to-date with their dance skills. When on the lookout for a second wife (his first having died only a year before), James Austen, Jane's eldest brother, worked on improving his dancing skills and assiduously went to every ball being held in the neighbourhood. 'A Ball is nothing without him', his sister remarked. James knew that a man who danced badly was seriously lessening his chances of attracting a wife.

Mr Collins lacks this vital knowledge. Either he has been badly taught, or he has failed to teach himself properly. It was a serious social lapse to dance badly. Thomas Wilson complains: 'a great number of Persons, who call themselves Dancers, and who are deemed so by others, are unworthy of that name'. This includes those who are out of time with the music, who shuffle and scrape, and tread on their partner's toes, and those 'bearing down the Hands of their Partner with all their Weight, whereby their Partner is obliged to stoop . . . of lifting the Arms of their Partners violently up and down . . . whereby they are always in laborious perpetual motion, producing the most disgusting Effect', or simply annoying one's partner 'with the noise of their feet'. Even if Mr Collins had only some of these deficiencies, it is no wonder that Elizabeth sat out further dances rather than endure the misery of dancing with him again.

Thomas Wilson

Thomas Wilson was an influential dancing master of the era. Based at the King's Theatre Opera House in London, and master of a dance academy in Holborn, he was well placed to write instruction manuals.

His first book was *An analysis of country dancing: wherein are displayed all the figures ever used in country dances, in a way so easy and familiar, that persons of the meanest capacity may in a short time acquire (without the aid of a master) a complete knowledge of that rational and polite amusement.* To which are added instructions for dancing some entire new reels; *together with the rules, regulations, and complete etiquette of the ball room.* It was popular because of its useful text and diagrams explaining the figures of the dances. Published in 1808, it was expanded and reissued in 1811, and then in 1815 was turned into *The Complete System of English Country Dancing.* He was the author of at least fifteen dance manuals, including *Quadrille Fan, Treasures of Terpsichore* and *The Art of Dancing.* His books remained in use until the 1850s.

Thomas Wilson regarded dancing as 'the most enchanting of all human amusements, it is the parent of joy, and the soul and support of cheerfulness; it banishes grief, cheers the evening hours of those who have studied or laboured in the day, and brings with it a mixture of delightful sensations which enrapture the senses'. Of course such comments from Thomas Wilson were not disinterested – he wanted people to buy his manuals and pay to attend his classes. And not all of Jane Austen's characters would agree that dancing always 'enraptured the senses' and 'banished sadness' – Edmund Bertram, Tom Bertram, Elizabeth Bennet and Catherine Morland for various reasons find themselves quite depressed at the end of an evening in the ballroom.

Jane Austen learns to dance

Jane Austen learned her first dance steps at Steventon. There, in the busy rectory, she was shown the patterns and movements of the dance by her mother and sister, and first practised them with her brothers. Probably Mrs Austen played dance tunes on the family harpsichord so her children could dance together. Was the 'best parlour' used for these important lessons, or was the furniture of the 'common parlour' pushed aside to make room? Henry Austen later remembered how Jane excelled in dance – perhaps he gave her some of those first lessons.

Once she had mastered the basics, young Jane had opportunities to dance in neighbourhood homes – the Lloyd sisters, Martha and Mary, came to live at nearby Deane when Jane was thirteen, just the right age for a girl to start thinking of balls. There were also six daughters in the Bigg family at Manydown. Jane Austen referred to a 'Child's Ball' held there in 1808. It's likely, with all those young people, that children's balls were a part of life at Manydown in the 1780s and 1790s. There Jane could have joined in the fun of learning new dance steps with friends she knew well.

Mr Austen was not a wealthy man – a dance master to provide private lessons for his daughters was probably out of his budget. But with an older sister and brothers, and with older friends and even parents who could all help her learn, Jane Austen, like the girls at Mrs Goddard's school, scrambled herself into 'a little dance education', and was soon ready to make a more formal appearance in a ballroom.

Dance as exercise

Dancing also provided one of the few ways in which young females could exercise. Horse riding hardly made a girl breathless, and walking at anything more than a gentle pace was frowned upon, but a ball could provide a good workout for the night. It certainly leaves Fanny Price gasping for breath and clutching her side, for the only other exercise she has is sitting on a horse and letting it take her for a gentle ride. Dancing brings on a cramp the next day in Harriet Smith, so she doesn't seem too used to exercise either, but Jane Austen found it kept her fit and healthy and she was proud of being able to dance the night away 'without any fatigue' when she was young. Pleasant music stimulated young people to action and a good evening's dancing could work up a healthy glow and help to get rid of some of those excess pounds which, in an age of heavy eating and drinking, piled on so quickly and made a Regency gown or tight breeches look unflattering. The Prince Regent, a fine dancer in his youth, was forced to give it up when his obesity gave him the nickname of 'Prince of Whales', even though he wore a corset in a ballroom.

Of course, dancing also provided exercise for those who were no longer young. Older people in need of physical exertion could continue to join the dance for many years. Mr Weston, probably going on sixty, is more than capable of leading Mrs Elton to the top of the dance and doing the honours with her.

‘An effective exhibition’ – dressing for the dance

‘I never in my life saw any thing more elegant than their dresses.’
PRIDE AND PREJUDICE

Elizabeth Bennet, preparing to dance with Mr Wickham at the Netherfield Ball, ‘dressed with more than usual care’. Like every young lady of that era, she knew that dressing well for a ball was one of the most important things an unmarried woman could do. Balls were a vital opportunity for display, for advertisement. As the fashion book *The Mirror of the Graces* reminded ladies, ‘As dancing is the accomplishment most calculated to display a fine form, elegant taste, and graceful carriage to advantage; so towards it our regards must be particularly turned: and we shall find that when Beauty in all her power is to be set forth, she cannot choose a more effective exhibition.’ Mary Russell Mitford wrote of women at dances: ‘they dress to marry’. While she did not approve, she recognized that dressing well for a ball was vital for any single woman. Catherine Morland, with a ball in Bath to look forward to, has only one thought: ‘What gown and what head-dress she should wear on the occasion became her chief concern.’

When a woman stood opposite a man in the dance set, he was distant enough to have a good view of her, but he was also close enough to touch, note an enticing glimpse of ankle as she skipped or jumped, and appreciate her figure as he spun her around on the dance floor. If a man was not dancing but merely watching from the sidelines, as Darcy does when he first appears in *Pride and Prejudice*, then he had an even better chance of ogling the females there. Mr Darcy does not have to make himself available as a dance partner (or as a husband, which is really what he is signalling when he refuses to dance), but can instead stand back and, as a voyeur, inspect the available talent until tempted by some Georgian beauty simply too appealing to resist. Women, only too aware of male gazes from nearby or from the edges of the ballroom, simply had to make the most of the opportunity for display. It was vital to look one's absolute best for a ball! One also had to be careful to stay looking good throughout the evening and avoid having fine clothes ruined. Wax dripping from candles in overhead lights on to delicate muslins or fine wigs was one hazard, horse dung outside in the streets which could damage a dainty slipper was another.

So what clothes would Elizabeth Bennet have donned 'with such care'? What would she have chosen with the aim of exhibiting her best qualities to the admiring eyes of Mr Wickham? Elizabeth's dress would have been made from a delicate and light fabric such as muslin or crepe de Chine. The wide petticoats and formal patterns of Mrs Bennet's youth had been abandoned and fabrics had been getting flimsier. Classical ideals were influencing fashion, with both men and women being made more statuesque and slender by their garments. Waistlines had moved upwards and styles grown more revealing. Doctors blamed light muslins and so much uncovered flesh for a rise in consumption – 'the muslin disease,' is what they called it. Probably Elizabeth's muslin dress was white (considered the most elegant colour for single ladies – Fanny Price wears white for her first ball), but it could have been pink or yellow, pale green or blue as light colours were also popular. Catherine Morland wears a 'sprigged muslin robe with blue trimmings'. Mrs Bennet comments excitedly on the dresses worn by Miss Bingley and Mrs Hurst: 'I never in my life saw anything more elegant than their dresses. I dare say the lace upon Mrs Hurst's gown – ', but Mr Bennet stops her before she can particularize. Men may not have wanted to hear details of ball dresses, but women were quick to notice the style, likely cost and detail of another woman's dress, especially if that woman were a rival.

Elizabeth's dress would also have had a train. These became a feature of evening gowns around 1800. Novelist Oliver Goldsmith commented on the fashion: 'As a lady's quality or fashion was once determined here by the circumference of her hoop, both are now measured by the length of her tail. Women of moderate fortunes are contented with tails moderately long; but ladies of true taste and distinction set no bounds to their ambition in this particular.' Miss Bingley, determined to impress with London fashions, is certain to have had a very long 'tail' to her dress. Trains needed some manipulation on the dance floor, especially with a clumsy partner such as Mr Collins, but many gowns had a small hoop or some other device allowing the train to be raised out of the way of awkward feet during the dance. Catherine Morland and Isabella Thorpe in *Northanger Abbey* pin up each other's trains before dancing in Bath. When not dancing, a lady could let her train down again. In *The Watsons* Mrs Edwards' satin train swishes gracefully 'along the clean floor of the ball-room'.

In Jane Austen's day necklines had dipped to reveal enticing glimpses of bosom. She was no prude, but she did not approve of the 'ugly naked shoulders' she saw at dances, or the exposed bosoms and the damp muslins. One suspects that Mr Bennet should have come out of the library to inspect Lydia's dress before she left for a ball. Well-grown, tall (she is the tallest of the Bennet sisters) and fully developed as she is, Lydia would be just the sort of female to show off her charms as brazenly and revealingly as possible. A low neckline would be guaranteed to draw the eye of every male in the vicinity.

Emma Watson of *The Watsons* discovers that 'the first bliss of a ball' is dressing for it. For poor Elizabeth Bennet, it is the *only* bliss. She dresses with care and excitement, believing she will be displaying her elegant figure, her taste in dress, and her pretty gown, to the appreciative eyes of Mr Wickham. Instead, she is tripped over by Mr Collins, lectured by Mr Darcy, and embarrassed by most of her own family.

Accessories

Gloves were always worn on formal occasions such as balls. Elizabeth could have purchased light fabric ones from the Meryton milliner. Gloves were usually white, but also came in pastel shades such as lemon and lilac. In 1798 Jane Austen purchased 'light and pretty' coloured gloves for herself and her sister at a cost of four shillings, but this price was so cheap she doubted their durability. When she did spend more, it took all her savings: 'All my money is spent in buying white gloves', she complained to her sister. Gloves made from soft kid or other leather were also available from a local glover or haberdasher (such as Ford's shop in *Emma*), but fabric ones were becoming more and more popular as they were considerably cheaper. Ingenious glove strings and buckles kept elbow-length gloves unwrinkled and neat during dancing.

As the Netherfield ball takes place in winter, shawls would have been required, especially at arrival or departure time. Shawls began to be worn at London dances in the 1780s. As well as providing warmth, they could, if nicely draped, add to the general elegance of an ensemble. Beautiful shawls were entering the market from the East Indies – Lady Bertram wants William Price to bring two such shawls back from his next voyage. Shawls were laid aside while dancing because arms needed to be free for the movements of the dance, and their gracefulness shown off at the same time.

Jane Austen provides few details of Elizabeth's appearance at any time in *Pride and Prejudice*, but she does tell the reader that the Bennet girls wear shoe-roses to the Netherfield ball. The actual shoes would have been simple, flat dancing slippers, probably with silk soles. They were not very sturdy and cases record ladies sometimes completely shredding their dancing slippers in one evening. Shoes were often made to match a particular dress and many a lady's workbox contained shoemaker's tools and accoutrements. Mrs Austen made dancing shoes for her granddaughters, but Jane Austen did not make her own and was 'not fond' even of ordering them. She liked her shoes to have totally flat heels, and she mentions owning shoes in green, white, black, blue and even pink. Shoes were often tied on round the ankle with ribbon, like the ballet shoes of today. Once made, the shoes had to be decorated (especially when hemlines began to rise in the 1810s). The Bennet girls order shoe-roses from Meryton (this has to be done 'by proxy' as bad weather prevents them from going into town to choose their own). A shoe-rose was made from a piece of ribbon tied up in a rosette pattern and attached to the front of the shoe. Jane Austen made shoe-roses from a 'black satin ribbon with a proper perl edge', which sounds very pretty and also luxurious (perl edging was a fancy looped stitch that was more expensive to make).

Stockings usually came to just above the knee, and of course a garter was required to hold them in place during dancing. A pretty piece of ribbon or little buckle often sufficed, but in the late eighteenth century a 'spring garter' was invented and became popular. Silk stockings were generally chosen for evening wear, usually white but sometimes with a blush of pink in them, and often embroidered with 'clocks' or dainty lace inserts. If one could not afford silk, there was a good range of cotton stockings available then in England, thanks to Arkwright's cotton mill. They were so good that, in spite of war, Empress Josephine of France ordered her stockings from England.

Elizabeth Bennet is young and marriageable, so is unlikely to have worn a cap. Probably her hair was curled by the family maid, then decorated with a bandeau or filet, or jewels (Miss Tilney has 'white beads round her head') or feathers. Naive Catherine Morland didn't recognize the white beads as pearls. She and her chaperone Mrs Allen, looking into a Bath ballroom, 'saw nothing of the dancers but the high feathers of some of the ladies'. A tastefully placed ostrich feather made a woman appear taller, attracted attention as it nodded with the movements of the dance, and also indicated wealth (the feathers had to be imported from South Africa).

Little jewellery was worn to balls. Mrs Elton is able to look complacently around the Crown Inn and remark: 'I see very few pearls in the room except mine', but she has a tendency to overdress. In 1800 the *Morning Post* announced amethyst and topaz to be 'preferable' to other jewels for young ladies. One year later Jane Austen had a topaz cross

to wear at balls, the gift of her brother Charles. Fanny Price's brother gives her an amber cross, which she wants to wear to her first ball.
Whether it should hang on a ribbon or a chain perplexes Fanny sorely,
and then when Mary Crawford and cousin Edmund both give her gold
chains, she is bewildered even more because she cannot choose between
them. It is symbolically fitting that Mary's chain (really a gift from her
brother Henry) does not fit through the ring of Fanny's cross, whereas

Edmund's chain fits perfectly. Fanny, however, is anxious to please and decides finally to hang both chains around her neck. Elizabeth Bennet has no brother or cousin to offer her such gifts – she probably dances at Netherfield unadorned by jewels. Mr Darcy clearly thinks that her 'fine eyes' provide sparkle enough!

A fan was an essential accessory in the ballroom. Elizabeth, angry with Mr Darcy when their dance together ends, can cool her flushed cheeks by fanning herself. Ballrooms were often hot and stuffy (Frank Churchill insists that windows do sometimes need to be flung open). Even at Mansfield Park the ballroom is airless and William Price works away 'as if for life' at fanning his partner's cheeks to cool her down. But the fan had many other attributes. It could be used for flirtation, drawing attention to fluttering eyelashes and welcoming glances; for avoidance (Catherine Morland 'kept her eyes intently fixed on her fan' so she wouldn't meet the eyes of John Thorpe); for noting down the names of the evening's partners, or a brief reminder to oneself of the steps of the dance (though this would only be done on a very cheap, disposable fan, or on an ivory or bone fan that could be cleaned off later). Fans were even used in the eighteenth century for conveying political messages. Author Joseph Addison, in an essay in *The Spectator*, noted that there was scarce an emotion that could not be conveyed by the fan – anger, amorousness, timidity, merriment, confusion. A lady skilled in the language of the fan could invite or dismiss a prospective partner and use it for flirtation or command. Writer Soame Jenyns asked admiringly about the fan:

> What verse can e'er explain its various parts
> Its numerous uses, motions, charms and arts?
> Its shake triumphant, its virtuous clap,
> Its angry flutter, and its wanton tap.

One can imagine Elizabeth's 'angry flutters' with her fan when Mr Darcy has annoyed her and Mr Wickham has let her down.

Male attire

Mr Wickham stays away from the Netherfield Ball, much to Elizabeth's disappointment. He is not anxious to encounter Mr Darcy there. Had he attended the event, he would have gone dressed in his formal army uniform. The red coats of the officers dancing at Netherfield would have made a bright splash of colour in the ballroom. This is why Lydia Bennet longs to get to the Brighton ballrooms, where the quartered regiment would ensure plenty of scarlet coats. But the newspaper *Lewes and Brighthelmstone Journal* feared that the preponderance of soldiers attracted too many of the Lydia Bennets of the Regency world, who would lower the tone of their assemblies 'when they expose themselves in dancing the Irish wriggle with any fellow in a bit of scarlet and a feather'. Scarlet coats were seen as attracting the female gaze and then deranging feminine minds by sheer physical magnetism. Mrs Edwards in *The Watsons* complains when her daughter Mary dances with officers instead of with the sons of her neighbours, but her husband quite reasonably counters her complaint by saying, 'But if these soldiers are quicker than other people in a Ball room, what are young ladies to do?'

> 'Elizabeth . . . looked in vain for Mr Wickham among the cluster of red coats there assembled'
> *Pride and Prejudice*

Mr Darcy and Mr Bingley, however, would have dressed in the formal men's attire expected at balls – knee breeches, silk stockings, flat leather shoes with decorative buckles, and a close-fitting frock coat in dark fabric, over a lighter and possibly more ornate waistcoat. White gloves were mandatory. A gentleman's hair, by this time, was his own and not a wig, as powder had gone out of fashion, except among older men – Mr Bennet, who owns a 'powdering gown', went to Netherfield with powdered hair.

Dress was strict for men when they attended balls. Thomas Wilson, in *A Companion to the Ball Room* (1816), insists that 'Gentlemen are not permitted to enter the Ball Room, in boots, spurs, gaiters, trousers, or with canes or sticks; nor are loose pantaloons considered proper for a Full Dress Ball.' The Duke of Wellington was once turned away from Almack's because his attire did not fit the rules of that select establishment.

Jane Austen dresses for a ball

Jane Austen wrote in *Northanger Abbey* that 'Dress is at all times a frivolous distinction', but she took just as much pleasure as does her heroine Catherine Morland in dressing for a ball. White seems to have been a favourite colour of hers (she wrote approvingly in 1801 of a Mrs and Miss Holder whose 'gowns look so white and nice') and she herself had white muslin made up for Bath balls.

Like her heroine Emma Woodhouse, Jane Austen had 'the highest value for elegance', so to make very sure her own dress was pretty and stylish, she consulted with friends and her sister: 'I cannot determine what to do about my new Gown; I wish such things were to be bought ready made. – I have some hopes of meeting Martha at . . . Deane next Tuesday, & shall see what she can do for me.' Jane Austen's nephew, James Edward Austen-Leigh, wrote in his *Memoir* of his aunt's enjoyment of sewing with friends: 'some of her merriest talk was over clothes which she and her companions were making.'

It distressed Jane Austen that she could not afford a new gown for each season's balls: 'I am so tired & ashamed of half my present stock that I even blush at the sight of the wardrobe that contains them.' To update her look, ball dresses had to be altered and adapted. In one instance she 'lowered the bosom, especially at the corners, and plaited black satin ribbon round the top'.

It is clear from her letters that she was fussy about stockings, greatly preferring 'having two pair only of that quality to three of an inferior sort'. In 1811 she purchased two pairs of just such fine stockings, made of silk, at Grafton House in London.

As Jane Austen grew older she preferred to wear a cap to balls. Caps saved a world of trouble in hairdressing, so she was very fond of them. A 'Mamalouc cap' (inspired by Horatio Nelson's Nile campaigns) and a black velvet one with a band of silver around it and a coquelicot feather, are two that she mentions wearing to dances. She and her sister borrowed and adapted each other's caps frequently.

Once neatly dressed and at a ball, Jane Austen delighted in noting the clothes of others. 'I am amused by the present style of female dress', she wrote from London on one visit to the capital. On all occasions she was observant of fashion trends: 'stays now are not made to force the Bosom up at all; – that was a very unbecoming, unnatural fashion. I was really glad to hear that they [dresses] are not to be so much off the shoulders as they were'.

No satisfactory portrait of Jane Austen exists. However, an 'imaginist' can picture her in a ballroom – elegantly clad in her simple white muslin gown, her legs in quality white stockings and on her head a cap she'd had made in London of 'white satin and lace, and a little white flower perking out of the left ear' – confident in her apparel, her large perceptive eyes amusedly watching for particularities in the dresses of others.

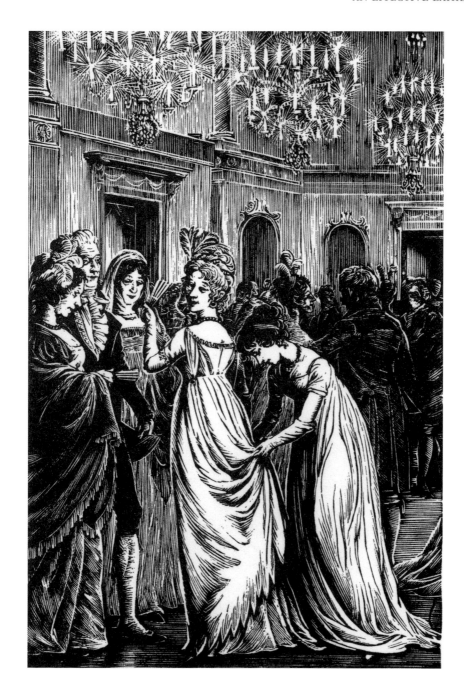

Getting to and from a ball

*'Therefore with three methods of going, I must have been more
at the Ball than anybody else.'*
Letter from Jane Austen, 1800

The Bennets have a carriage to transport the entire family to the ball at Netherfield. The horses, used for farm work during the day, were probably not happy to be taken out of their stables on a cold night, but at least Elizabeth can travel in comfort to the event, with no worry about how to get home again. Other Jane Austen heroines are not so fortunate.

A carriage was a luxury item, and not every family could afford to buy one, let alone purchase or rent the horses, provide accommodation and food for them, and employ a groom. Many a young lady anxious to attend a ball was at the mercy of neighbours. If they offered a lift, or an overnight stay, she could attend her ball; but if they forgot to extend such an offer, she must stay at home.

Emma Watson, of *The Watsons*, is in just such a position. To attend her first assembly ball in the Surrey 'town of D.', she has to be driven three miles to get there: 'her eldest sister, whose delight in a ball was not lessened by ten years' enjoyment, had some merit in cheerfully undertaking to drive her and all her finery in the old chair to D. on the important morning'. Elizabeth Watson is not able to attend the ball because someone in the family has to stay at home to look after old Mr Watson for the evening. She drives her sister Emma in the 'old chair' (i.e. a very simple open cart, with no lining or springs, which jolts along the road on two wheels), pulled by 'an old mare' who trots heavily along the country roads. Emma then has to impose on the hospitality of Mr and Mrs Edwards, people she has never met before, for a night's accommodation when the ball ends.

Poor Emma then has trouble getting home the next day. The family cart is needed elsewhere and although fashionable Tom Musgrave offers her a lift home in his curricle, she does not like to accept his offer. To be seen by half the inhabitants of the town perched in a sporty rig with a rakish young man she barely knows would not be good for Emma's reputation. Yet she cannot ask Mrs Edwards to provide her with a ride home in the Edwards' carriage; she can only hope for an offer, and Emma has some uncomfortable moments while she waits.

Even when a ride was promised, it could not always be relied on. Mr and Mrs Elton are supposed to take Miss Bates and Jane Fairfax to the ball at the Crown Inn. They forget to pick up the two ladies: 'The mistake had been slight. The carriage was sent for them now.' In this case, the ballroom is nearby so the mistake matters little, but many a young lady must have sat at home 'all dressed up with nowhere to go' because transport arrangements had been muddled or forgotten.

Once a young lady had accepted a lift, she had no say as to when she could arrive at the ball or when she could leave it. Emma Watson is forced to arrive too early because Mrs Edwards wants to 'get a good place by the fire'. Mrs Edwards doesn't want to be the very first – she waits until she hears the carriage of the Tomlinson family go by, 'which was the constant signal for Mrs Edwards to order hers to the door', but still they all arrive too early and find the room cold and empty. Emma feels awkward waiting for it to fill up. The Edwards family is also amongst the last to leave. Emma has no voice in these arrangements and her comfort and inclination are not consulted. The Edwards' home is only a few minutes' walk from the inn where the ball is held, but for a young woman to walk home unaccompanied was not an option. Indeed, it was rare for anyone to walk to or from a ball – if one had a carriage, it was always put into use on such occasions. The Coles live only a minute or two from the Crown Inn, but

they go there in their carriage nevertheless.

Elizabeth Bennet feels trapped at the end of the Netherfield ball but, like Emma Watson, can do nothing about it: 'The Longbourn party were the last of all the company to depart; and by a manoeuvre of Mrs Bennet had to wait for their carriages a quarter of an hour after every body else was gone, which gave them time to see how heartily they were wished away by some of the family.' No doubt Jane and Mr Bingley are happy 'standing together, a little detached from the rest', which is what Mrs Bennet has schemed for, but Elizabeth is silent and unhappy and longing to be at home. Transport arrangements were rarely made to suit single females!

Jane Austen travels to the ball

Jane Austen knew only too well how difficult it could sometimes be to get to a ball. Unlike Cinderella, she had no fairy godmother who could turn a pumpkin into a golden coach, although she must often have wished for one. For some time in the 1790s her father kept a carriage, but it proved too expensive, and in 1798 he gave it up. This meant that Jane Austen was dependent on friends, or even her own feet. In Kent she once walked home from a family dance, even though it was raining. It was eight miles from her Steventon home to Basingstoke – too far to walk if she wished to attend the assembly balls regularly held there.

Sometimes Jane Austen was lucky with travel arrangements: 'On wednesday morning it was settled that Mrs Harwood, Mary & I should go together, & shortly afterwards a very civil note of invitation for me came from Mrs Bramston, who wrote I beleive as soon as she knew of the Ball. I might likewise have gone with Mrs Lefroy, & therefore with three methods of going, I must have been more at the Ball than anybody else.' On this occasion in 1800 she was overwhelmed with offers, but she still had to make arrangements to sleep the night with the Harwoods at Deane and get home from there the next day. And she still had to feel obliged and dependent. It was not always easy constantly being made to feel grateful.

Balls on moonlit nights

'It was moonlight and everyone was full of engagements.'
SENSE AND SENSIBILITY

Balls were usually planned to take place when there was a full moon. This meant that your invited guests had more natural light for the journey, which lessened the risk of carriage accidents. Moonlight also made travellers slightly safer from highwaymen, who preferred dark nights for their work. When Sir John Middleton in *Sense and Sensibility* wants to host an event at the time of the full moon, he finds all his neighbours have done likewise.

Returning from a dinner Party at Night!
June. 12th 1816.

Getting to the ball on public transport

Catherine Morland, off to the Upper Rooms in Bath in *Northanger Abbey*, has to take public transport. Private carriages were little used within Bath, except for excursions into the countryside. Within the city one took a 'chair'.

Sedan chairs, invented in the French town of the same name, came to Bath in the seventeenth century. They varied in design – some were roofless, others had roofs that could be raised to make space for tall headdresses, some had front doors, and others side doors. The chair structure was raised on two long poles and carried by two strong fellows, 'chairmen', through the streets of Bath, right into the front door of the Upper Rooms themselves. Jane Austen does not inform her readers as to the exact style of chair that Catherine uses. It could have been a conventional sedan chair, or it could have been the one invented in 1780 by Arthur Dawson, equipped with wheels, which made a lot of noise as they went over the cobbles. These eventually resulted in sedan chairs disappearing, but not until well into the nineteenth century.

After problems with chairmen holding passengers for ransom and fighting with their chair poles, Bath's social arbiter Beau Nash imposed discipline upon them. Chairmen had to register with the local magistrate, and they had to charge fixed rates (based on time, distance and the number of hills to be climbed). In 1793 there was an attempt to introduce a single charge, but the chairmen rioted and the proposal was dropped. Catherine's journey from Great Pulteney Street to the Upper Rooms would have cost her between one shilling and six pence and two shillings (one way) – an expensive luxury at the time.

She would not, however, have found her chair particularly luxurious. Like modern taxis, the chairs remained outside in all weather, sometimes with the chairmen asleep inside them. Matthew Bramble in Smollett's novel *Humphry Clinker* complains that sedan chairs were 'boxes of wet leather', with their 'linings impregnated with so many sponges'. However, Catherine, returning from a ball where she has danced with Henry Tilney, is too happy to notice damp linings or leather: 'she cheerfully submitted to the wish of Mr Allen, which took them rather early away, and her spirits danced within her, as she danced in her chair all the way home'.

She felt the awkwardness of having no party to join.

Assembly balls

*'I have charged my Myrmidons to send me an account of the Basingstoke Ball;
I have placed my spies at different places.'*
Letter from Jane Austen, 1800

Enter the handsome hero – tall, rich, noble, and gorgeous, but too proud for his company. Enter the lovely heroine – spirited, clever, but in want of a dance partner. Bring them together and make sparks fly when he refuses to dance with her. This of course is Jane Austen's recipe for one of the most important scenes in *Pride and Prejudice*. It is impossible to imagine the novel without the Meryton assembly ball where all this occurs.

Elizabeth Bennet is not Jane Austen's only heroine to meet her future husband at an assembly ball. Catherine Morland meets Henry Tilney at one in Bath, Emma Watson meets her Mr Howard at a public dance, and Anne Elliot's first encounter with Captain Wentworth could possibly have taken place at a Somerset assembly room. Assembly balls were the foremost courtship arena of the day. Now, young men and women head to nightclubs to dance and hopefully fall in love, just as Regency ladies and gentlemen hurried to assembly rooms across the country, anxious to meet the partner of their dreams. Assembly balls provided not only an opportunity to meet someone new, but also the chance to touch, talk, flirt and ogle. Balls were much, much more than simply venues for dancing.

Throughout the reign of George III towns all over England were hosting assembly balls. A large inn, public building or town hall would serve as venue, tickets were issued, notices inserted in local papers, musicians hired, and the ball held. Any town with the least pretension to fashion and a respectably sized middle-class population had to hold assembly balls.

Because they were open to anyone who could purchase a subscription ticket, they attracted an uncontrolled social array. Mrs Robert Watson refuses to attend the Croydon assemblies because they are 'rather too mixed'. Jane Austen once complained of the 'ungenteel' attendees encountered by one of her brothers at a Gosport assembly, while the Bath assembly balls attracted the likes of vulgar Isabella Thorpe and her brother, John. Generally they were attended by men of the rising middle classes – clergy, lawyers, soldiers, merchants: respectable people who wanted their sons and daughters to have fun and find suitable marriage partners in the process.

Nobility, however, were expected to patronize such events held in their neighbourhoods. The Hampshire aristocracy – the Dorchesters, the Boltons, and the Earl and Countess of Portsmouth – all made appearances at the Basingstoke assemblies of Jane Austen's youth. Mrs Austen was not impressed on one occasion when Lord and Lady Dorchester failed to appear. She expressed her disapproval in verse:

> It would have been a better dance
> But for the following circumstance;
> The Dorchesters, so high in station,
> Dined out that day, by invitation.

In *The Watsons*, the Osbornes of Osborne Castle see it as their duty to patronize the D. assembly (Lord Osborne 'came, in fact, only because it was judged expedient to please the Borough'), and the locals all feel it adds a certain cachet to the event when nobility graces it with their presence: 'their coming gives a credit to our assembly. The Osbornes, being known to have been at the first ball, will dispose a great many people to attend the second. It is more than they deserve; for, in fact, they add nothing to the pleasure of the evening: they come so late, and go so early; – but great people have always their charm.' Mr Bingley clearly feels that, as a new tenant of one of the big houses near Meryton, he must go to the assembly there, not only as a pleasure, but as an obligation to the neighbourhood.

The assembly ball in *The Watsons*

Nowhere in Jane Austen's fiction is any ball described in such detail and at such length as the one held on Tuesday, 13 October at D.'s White Hart Inn in *The Watsons*. It is the subject of the novel's opening line, it is well discussed by several major characters before it happens, a big effort is made by the heroine to physically get to it, the order of arrivals is listed, the ball itself depicted, the departures described and, finally, post-mortems follow the next day. Jane Austen achieves a great deal with this assembly ball, filling the public space with characters who have a variety of reasons for being there, and who respond very differently to the night's events.

The ball is, of course, Emma Watson's 'debut', her 'coming out' in the town of D. Having spent much of her life living far away with a wealthy aunt, she has been forced back home upon that aunt's marriage, so the ball is 'her first public appearance in the neighbourhood'. She goes feeling, as a stranger, that her 'enjoyment therefore must be very doubtful', and is concerned about staying with the Edwards family whom she hardly knows. Soon after entering the ballroom, however, Emma is looked at with admiration and interest: 'A new face, and a very pretty one, could not be slighted – her name was whispered from one party to another.' An officer asks her to dance, and Emma begins to enjoy the ball.

Jane Austen, however, has plans to introduce her heroine to her hero during this ball and has to somehow bring together a man belonging to the aristocratic Osborne party and the daughter of an impoverished clergyman. The ingenious device she employs is a child – young Charles Blake. By rescuing him from his disappointment and embarrassment at being stood up by Miss Osborne, Emma attracts the notice of Charles's family and friends – his mother, uncle, Tom Musgrave, Lady Osborne and Lord Osborne: 'Oh! Uncle, do look at my partner. She is so pretty!' young Charles announces loudly. What heroine could ask for a better recommendation to the hero? Mr Howard and Charles's mother, Mrs Blake, ask to be introduced to her, and Mr Howard invites Emma to dance, but they are then 'immediately impelled in opposite directions' by the pressure of the crowd in the room. Movement is used

here to foreshadow the future progress of this romance – Emma's father will soon die and this will result
in Emma's removal to Croydon. Mr
Howard does manage to return to
claim her hand in time for the dance,
as he will finally get to Emma's side
to propose marriage (or that, at least,
was Jane Austen's plan for this unfinished novel). The enjoyment with
which they dance together also indicates the promise of compatibility in
their eventual marriage.

The ball also brings the first appearance of the Osbornes. Lord Osborne is 'a very fine young man; but
there was an air of coldness, of care-
lessness, even of awkwardness about
him, which seemed to speak him out
of his element in a ball room . . . he
was not fond of women's company,
and he never danced'. The phrase 'he
never danced' is enough to assure the
reader that he will never be Emma's
hero. In fact, Lord Osborne is the antithesis of a hero – he stands 'quite
alone' at the end of the room, 'as if retreating as far as he could from the
ball, to enjoy his own thoughts and gape without restraint'. He then tries
to persuade his friend Tom Musgrave to dance with Emma so that he
can stand by and watch, and when she dances with Mr Howard instead,
Lord Osborne jostles Mr Howard's elbow, so close does he stand to stare
at the dancing couple. There is something decidedly odd about this
young Lord – is he a voyeur or a sort of Peeping Tom of the ballroom?

Tom Musgrave's ballroom appearance is also made to look dubi-
ous by Jane Austen. He lurks in the passage waiting for the important

Osbornes to arrive, he leaves when they do but only to go into another room of the inn, he flirts with Emma as he has flirted with all her sisters in turn, he blithely tells several fibs, and he toadies shamelessly to the Osbornes. Tom Musgrave is piqued by Emma's lack of interest in him; he is clearly unused to thinking of anyone except himself. Jane Austen contrasts his bad ballroom manners and selfish vapidity and Lord Osborne's cold voyeurism with the intelligence and gentlemanliness of Mr Howard.

Other characters come vividly alive in this assembly ball: Mrs Edwards, rather snobbish and eager for her daughter Mary *not* to dance too often with the officers; Mr Edwards, enjoying good luck in the adjoining card room ('he had won four rubbers out of five'); not to mention thoughtless Miss Osborne, who breaks her engagement to dance with an excited boy so that she can dance with a colonel instead. Handsome Lady Osborne, kind Mrs Blake, proud Miss Carr, the energetic officers and the various others who make up the 'happy dancers' move about the White Hart ballroom, its 'broad entrance-passage', card and supper rooms – they are all as real as life. Those present in the scene comment on the success of the occasion, and Jane Austen herself must have known that, in her manuscript pages of this novel, she had created 'an excellent ball'.

The assembly balls in *Northanger Abbey*

No Jane Austen heroine does as much dancing as Catherine Morland of *Northanger Abbey*. On five separate occasions she dances at assembly balls in Bath. These balls achieve a lot within the novel: they introduce her to Henry Tilney and further their knowledge of each other, they allow her to meet and form a close friendship with his sister Eleanor, they expose Isabella Thorpe for the shameless flirt she is, and they serve as a device in this novel to spoof Gothic literature.

Catherine's first, third and fourth Bath assembly balls all take place at the Upper Rooms (Jane Austen never informs her readers where Catherine's fifth ball is held, so it could also be in the Upper Rooms). These Upper Rooms, setting for Catherine's 'debut' appearance in Bath, were northwest of Queen's Square. Their erection in 1771, from plans drawn up by John Wood the Younger, was financed (the rooms cost £20,000) by a company of Bath shareholders, and they became immediately popular with locals and visitors alike. Very soon they had eclipsed the earlier built Lower Rooms in popularity and extra card and billiard rooms

> '**The important evening came which was to usher her into the Upper Rooms.**'
> *Northanger Abbey*

had to be added. The place was soon a showcase for the well-bred and the fashionably dressed – the 'beautiful people' of the Regency world. Attendees arrived through two carriage entrances at the large paved area out front, and proceeded indoors to the 100-foot-long room with its five gorgeous crystal chandeliers glittering overhead. Tradesmen were excluded, strict dress and behaviour codes drawn up, and tickets issued. Maintaining class barriers, however, proved to be something of a problem. As the decades passed and the number of attendees grew, more and more of those 'whose dress and station in life does not entitle them to associate with people of distinction' infiltrated the events. There were even complaints that servants were creeping in! By the time Catherine Morland dances there, the uncontrolled social mix and numbers were becoming hard to handle. When she arrives there on 'that important evening' of her first Bath ball 'the season was full, the room crowded'.

In fact, Jane Austen describes the crowd as a 'mob', requiring Catherine and her chaperone Mrs Allen to make their way through all its possible dangers (such risks as damaged finery and dresses 'torn asunder') with 'necessary caution' and 'continued exertion of strength and ingenuity'. The rooms are so packed that Catherine cannot even get a proper view of them to search out handsome young men as potential partners. All she can see are high feathers on the tops of ladies' heads. The two women have to squeeze out for tea, get wearied by 'being continually pressed' by people and, worst of all, she finds no partner. She goes to a ball and she does not dance a single dance! The event is presented by Jane Austen with light irony as a form of 'imprisonment' and near-torture. Just as Gothic heroines in the fiction Catherine loves to read are locked away and ill-treated in dungeons, so Catherine is trapped and pressed by this assembly ball crowd.

Upper Room balls finished promptly at 11 p.m. (even if everyone was mid-dance, so strict was the rule), but poor Catherine is longing for her bed well before then. When the dancing stops 'the company

began to disperse . . . enough to leave space for the remainder to walk about in some comfort; and now was the time for a heroine, who had not yet played a very distinguished part in the events of the evening, to be noticed and admired'. After Catherine hears that 'two gentlemen pronounced her to be a pretty girl', she goes home happy at the end of this otherwise disappointing ball.

Bath's Lower Rooms, dating from 1708, were older than the Upper ones (which were sometimes referred to as the New Rooms). Situated in the lower part of town, they no longer exist, having burned down in 1820. All that remains today is a section of portico and exterior walls. Ninety feet long with fine river views, the Lower Rooms struggled to keep up with the competition of the Upper Rooms and grew shabby and unfashionable, despite their convenient position. But in 1784 the owners put forward a new subscription package of fourteen dress balls and twenty cotillion balls. Popular Mr James King took over as master of ceremonies and remained in that post until 1805. It is Mr King who introduces Catherine to a young man called Henry Tilney. At first Catherine is unsure what to make of her new partner – she hardly understands his arch quizzing, is puzzled whether or not to laugh, and finds his knowledge of muslins 'strange'. Yet, 'when the assembly closed, [they] parted on the lady's side at least, with a strong inclination for continuing the

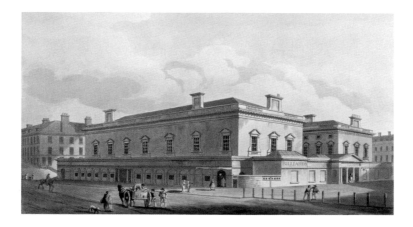

acquaintance'. The romance of *Northanger Abbey* is underway.

Catherine's connection with the Upper Rooms seems doomed to disappointment, however. On her second visit there she is ardently hoping to dance with Henry Tilney, introduced to her in the Lower Rooms about ten days before. Accompanied by the Allens once again, she also on this occasion has the Thorpes and her brother James along. Although John Thorpe has pre-engaged her for the first two dances, he wanders off to the card room, leaving Catherine with Isabella. Every proper Gothic heroine gets abandoned at some point in her career and this is Catherine's moment of desertion. Isabella hurries off to dance with James, and Catherine is left suffering with fortitude as a heroine should, but humiliated and miserable, all the same. The 'severe mortification' is increased when Henry Tilney approaches and invites her to dance, but she is forced by the pre-engagement to refuse him. When John Thorpe finally arrives and leads her to the set, she is 'separated from all her party, and away from all her acquaintance'. Thorpe's conversation is tiresome, Henry's request is not repeated, and she again ends the 'very dull' evening 'disappointed and vexed'.

But the cotillion ball described in chapter 10 of *Northanger Abbey*, which is also held at the Upper Rooms, goes some way to atone for the previous ones. It begins with difficulties – she is 'chiefly anxious' to avoid John Thorpe, lest he should engage her again, and is frightened that Henry Tilney will not. 'Every young lady may feel for my heroine in this critical moment', Jane Austen states feelingly (she must have known such ballroom awkwardnesses herself!) 'for every young lady has at some time or other known the same agitation. All have been, or at least all have believed themselves to be, in danger from pursuit of some one whom they wished to avoid; and all have been anxious for the attentions of some one whom they wished to please.' Jane Austen has put her heroine through various mock-Gothic trials – imprisonment, abandonment and shame. Now she must suffer 'the pursuit' and Catherine has to sit through the cotillions that open the ball trying desperately to escape Thorpe's notice, condemning herself for her folly and undergoing 'agony' in the process. Jane Austen makes these balls provide torments

for a heroine as exquisite as any depicted in the pages of Mrs Radcliffe's Gothic horror novels, and decidedly more realistic.

And then Catherine is saved! Henry Tilney, like a knight on a charger, conquers the crowd and is before her, soliciting her hand. But the villain of the piece continues to lurk and harm her: John Thorpe moves behind her in the dance, pesters her with his complaints, wearies her with his boorish behaviour, and irritates her partner. Finally he is 'born off by the resistless pressure of a long string of passing ladies'. Just as Jane Austen emasculated Lord Osborne in the White Hart ballroom, so she here demolishes Thorpe's masculinity when she shows him being swept away by women. Henry Tilney can part a crowd to get to the partner of his choice, but John Thorpe is enfeebled merely by dancing ladies. Catherine is then free to enjoy a spirited conversation with Henry comparing dance to marriage and afterwards to have all the felicity of an invitation to walk out with his sister. Little wonder that she dances in her chair as she rides through the town to Pulteney Street.

Northanger Abbey's final ball is given no specific location. Its Gothic motif is 'treachery'. Isabella Thorpe, by now engaged to Catherine's brother James, spends the evening flirting with Captain Tilney in James's absence. Catherine begins to grow aware of the falseness of her friend in this scene. She 'enjoyed her usual happiness with Henry Tilney' and goes down the short set with him 'listening with sparkling eyes to everything he said; and, in finding him irresistible, becoming so herself', and yet she is disappointed in her friend, and Isabella's dishonest disclaimers about her own behaviour unsettle Catherine and astonish her.

In five weeks in Bath, Catherine has danced at five assembly balls. The occasions have subjected her to a delightful range of spoof Gothic threats and dangers; they have introduced her to a 'not quite handsome' hero and given her opportunities to dance with him, they have exposed John Thorpe for the thug he is and his sister for a hardened and mercenary flirt. *Persuasion*, Jane Austen's other Bath novel, offers its reader no balls, so it is to *Northanger Abbey* that we must turn for charming depictions of Bath residents at play in assembly balls.

Jane Austen dances at an assembly ball

Jane Austen loved going to assembly balls. As an excited seventeen-year-old she began to attend those held in Basingstoke, eight miles from her Steventon home. These were held at the town hall, and there she danced on the first-floor ballroom, socializing with local families such as the

The Fancy Ball at the Upper Rooms Bath.

Terrys, Dummers, Bramstons and Lefroys. Her parents paid an annual subscription for the tickets, and the whole family enjoyed going. Mr Austen could play cards in the adjoining card room or discuss the price of crops with local squires, and Mrs Austen could catch up on local news with her friends, just as Mrs Bennet does with hers. Basingstoke offered several public balls each winter (between 1792 and 1801 more than fifty such balls were held there) and also offered 'extra' events – a 'club ball' in October, and a King's ball on George III's birthday. The organizers were the proprietors of local coaching inns who could expect to reap financial rewards for their efforts in the form of carriage hire, stabling, and waiting on servants needing food and drink.

Jane Austen enjoyed these balls so much that she was disappointed if she had had to miss one. If she was away from home, then she placed her 'spies' so as to get all the news. Catherine Bigg could be relied on to share gossip about who had danced with whom, who had too much to drink, which lady had opened the dance, and all the other juicy titbits of news the evening could provide. Jane Austen tried to ensure her absences from home did not clash with assembly dates: 'I would not on any account do so uncivil a thing by the Neighbourhood as to set off at that very time for another place.'

Was she nervous when she first put in an appearance there? A first ball could be a daunting experience for a young lady, but, if she did initially tremble slightly in her dance shoes, she soon overcame those nerves and relished the Basingstoke balls. Mrs Mitford, mother of the novelist Mary Russell Mitford, recalled seeing Jane Austen willing to stand up with anyone who asked her, and castigated her for this by describing her as 'a husband-hunting butterfly'. But if young Jane was asked to dance, and turned down the invitation, she would have then been forced to refuse every other man who asked her and sit out the dances at the side of the room. For a girl who loved dancing as much as young Jane Austen, this was hardly an option. And Mrs Mitford had a very plain daughter who was rarely asked to dance, so this was probably sour grapes on her part.

Family visits to other parts of the country gave Jane opportunities to dance at assembly balls in Deal, Lyme (where the rooms almost jutted out over the ocean at the bottom of Broad Street), Canterbury, Ashford, Bath, Faversham and Southampton (in the Dolphin Inn, still there today). As a visitor, not a local, she suffered anxieties over not being introduced to enough young men to ensure partners for the evening, but she also had the exciting possibility of meeting Mr Right. In Lyme she once had to sit out the first two dances, then be grateful to a Miss Armstrong for introducing her to a Mr Granville who asked for her hand in the dance. She also had to endure being ogled by an odd-looking man who didn't end up dancing with her, which made her feel very uncomfortable. And she never did meet Mr Right at an assembly ball. By the time she attended those held in Southampton she was in her early thirties and, while still as keen a dancer as ever, she realistically accepted that partners would be in short supply. 'You will not expect to hear that I was asked to dance', she wrote to her sister Cassandra, 'but I was.' At the Queen's Ball held there in 1809 she was asked to dance once, but was starting to feel that 'the trouble of dressing & going & being weary before it was half over' (as she commented of an Ashford ball) was not worth it when one watched instead of taking part.

Assembly balls were an important part of Jane Austen's social life. She may not have met the right man at such an event, but she certainly had a lot of fun in assembly rooms, seeing friends and neighbours, meeting new people, and joining in the fun of dancing at what was very much a local community event.

Masters of ceremonies

George and Cassandra Austen, Jane Austen's parents, married in Bath in 1864. If they danced there together in the days leading up to their wedding, they would have done so abiding by the rules and regulations established by Beau Nash. When their daughter Jane danced in Bath many years later, Nash's rules for conduct in the Bath assembly rooms still applied with very few changes.

Beau Nash was born in Wales and educated at Oxford. After he served in the army he was called to the bar, but neither career was a success. A dandy from an early age, he soon drew attention with his diamond shoe buckles, velvet coats and gold-lace ruffles. When he went to Bath he attracted the notice of the master of ceremonies and became his assistant. When that man was killed in a duel, Nash took on the role himself in 1704. Bath was then rising in importance as a place for the smart set and Nash played a vital role in making it the most fashionable city in England outside of London. During the eighteenth century, the city's population grew from 2000 to 30,000, and much of this increase was due to Nash. Nash levied a subscription on all visitors, arranged for new assembly rooms to be built, forbade private parties, and decided on starting and finishing times for Bath events. He insisted that all lodging houses be renovated to required standards and charged the tariffs he himself had set. He made it clear that swearing was out of order, set rules about the right clothes to wear, and arranged for the ringing of bells to greet distinguished visitors arriving in the city.

Nash's own behaviour was far from correct: he enjoyed keeping strings of mistresses; he was a chronic gambler; and he went deep into debt from gambling and his taste for expensive clothes. As master of ceremonies it was his job to match up young ladies with suitable dancing partners, to greet new arrivals to the city, and to pay the musicians at the end of the night. He even brokered marriages. He tried to protect gamblers from predatory cardsharps and he wouldn't allow men to wear their swords in the public rooms of Bath, which did help to stop the duels and violence. Nash broke down some of the formality of Bath society, allowing more middle class people to come to public balls (people like the Thorpes in *Northanger Abbey*).

Nash died in poverty in 1761. His debts had been so great that he had been forced to move in with his current mistress, Juliana Popjoy. She was so devastated by his death that she could no longer bear to live in the house without him and moved into a large hollowed-out tree nearby. Only when her own death was approaching did Juliana move out of her tree and back into a more normal residence. Bath Abbey has a plaque to Beau Nash, but it is really the city of Bath itself that is his true monument.

⅋

Nash had written up a code of conduct for the assembly rooms, and a generation later those rules were updated by James King, and were then in use for the next thirty years. Mr James King was master of ceremonies at the Lower Rooms from 1785 to 1805 (he then moved to the same position at the Upper Rooms). He held a distinguished war record from his time serving in America – perhaps military discipline and order helped him maintain decency and decorum in the ballroom. It was not for nothing that he was sometimes known around town as 'the King'.

His position was a prestigious and important one but, of all the duties Mr King ever performed, his most important was entirely imaginary – the introduction of Catherine Morland and Henry Tilney: 'the master of the ceremonies introduced to her a very gentlemanlike young man as a partner'. Later Henry mentions this master of ceremonies by name, when he tells Catherine how she ought to record their introduction in her journal: 'I danced with a very agreeable young man, introduced by Mr King.'

The assembly ball in *Pride and Prejudice*

In his *An Analysis of Country Dancing*, dance instructor Thomas Wilson asks: 'What place is so proper as the assembly-room to see the fashions and manners of the times, to study men and characters, to become accustomed to receive flattery without regarding it, to learn good breeding and politeness without affectation, to see grace without wantonness, gaiety without riot, dignity without haughtiness, and freedom without levity?' Yet when 'Mr Bingley, his two sisters, the husband of the eldest, and another young man' (who is, of course, Mr Darcy) enter the assembly room at Meryton, is this really what they find there?

Fortunately for the plot of *Pride and Prejudice*, it is not. While 'fashions and manners of the times' are on display, there is a very memorable lapse of 'good breeding'. Mr Darcy 'danced only once with Mrs Hurst and once with Miss Bingley, declined being introduced to any other lady, and spent the rest of the evening in walking about the room . . . His character was decided. He was the proudest, most disagreeable man in the world, and every body hoped that he would never come there again.' Darcy's ballroom behaviour is shockingly short of the 'good breeding and politeness' expected by Thomas Wilson. Sitting in that Meryton ballroom are young ladies without partners, and by parading about the room, Darcy publicly exhibits the fact that they do not attract him.

And then, he memorably insults the heroine, Elizabeth Bennet:

'Come, Darcy,' said [Bingley], 'I must have you dance. I hate to see you standing about by yourself in this stupid manner. You had much better dance.'

'I certainly shall not. You know how I detest it, unless I am particularly acquainted with my partner. At such an assembly as this, it would be insupportable. Your sisters are engaged, and there is not another woman in the room, whom it would not be a punishment to me to stand up with.'

When Bingley offers to introduce his friend to the sister of his partner, Jane Bennet, Darcy replies:

'Which do you mean?' and turning round he looked for a moment at Elizabeth, till catching her eye, he withdrew his own and coldly said, 'She is tolerable; but not handsome enough to tempt me; and I am in no humour at present to give consequence to young ladies who are slighted by other men.'

So poor Elizabeth is very far from receiving 'flattery without regarding it' in this ballroom – indeed, quite the opposite. She has to try and laugh herself out of it, but she is hurt by his remarks. Mr Darcy's insult comes from 'dignity with haughtiness'. Neither Elizabeth nor Thomas Wilson approve and it is clear that Darcy badly needs to be taught a lesson.

The politeness and good manners are, on this occasion, all left to Mr Bingley, who proves a positive model of ballroom deportment: 'Mr Bingley had soon made himself acquainted with all the principal people in the room; he was lively and unreserved, danced every dance, was angry that the ball closed so early, and talked of giving one himself at Netherfield. Such amiable qualities must speak for themselves.' Bingley will have other lessons to learn in the course of the novel, but an improvement in manners is not one of them. He does his duty by the neighbourhood in attending and by dancing with the two daughters of former Meryton mayor, Sir William Lucas; but he also pleases himself by dancing, twice, with Jane Bennet, and with her sister Elizabeth. Perhaps it is also the case that Mr Darcy needs to learn lessons in self-confidence. Is he diffident about his prowess as a dancer, or is he reluctant to expose himself to fortune-hunting girls and their ambitious mothers? Whatever his reasons, Darcy cannot walk out on to the Meryton dance floor in the easy, relaxed way his friend is able to.

Thomas Wilson stressed that an assembly ball must display 'grace

> 'When the party entered the assembly room, it consisted of … Mr Bingley, his two sisters, the husband of the eldest, and another young man.'
> *Pride and Prejudice*

without wantonness, gaiety without riot'. As the younger Bennet girls, Lydia and Kitty, are present at the Meryton assembly, it is doubtful whether wantonness and riot are avoided. The two girls 'had been fortunate enough to be never without partners', but later specimens of Lydia's behaviour are an indication of the indecorum and loudness she must have displayed at the Meryton ball.

Mr Bennet does not attend – he stays at home in his library, as perhaps he felt his preference for a study of 'men and characters' would not be gratified. It is a serious dereliction of his duties as a parent. Mr Bennet ought to be there, making discreet enquiries about the men who partner his daughters, restraining the worst of Lydia's excesses, and toning down the vulgarity of his wife. His indolence makes him miss an extremely important event: the introduction of his two future sons-in-law, one of whom behaves well and one who does not. Mr Darcy is proud and wounds Elizabeth's pride. He is prejudiced against his company even before he enters the room; she is prejudiced against him by the time she leaves it. The Meryton assembly ball is the catalyst of all the action and misunderstandings that follow and the setting for one of the most famous and loved scenes in all of literature.

.

Almack's assembly balls

Jane Austen never danced at Almack's in London, and neither do any of her characters. Most of them are not grand enough. Anne de Bourgh might have done so, had her health permitted, and had her mother bothered to take her to London for the season. But the Dashwood girls, Jane Bennet, the Steele sisters and even Mary Crawford all lacked the necessary social cachet and connections to gain entrance to these most exclusive balls.

Almack's was on King Street behind St James's Square and around the corner from White's club (visited by Henry Austen). First established in 1763 by Scot William Macall (the name was arrived at by reversing the two syllables of his name), Almack's offered balls and suppers once a week during the twelve weeks of the London season. Its balls were staid and its suppers frugal and stodgy, but still it was the Mecca of every marriageable young woman and her mama. There a young lady could dance with the most eligible bachelors in the land.

HIGHEST LIFE IN LONDON. *Tom & Jerry "Sporting a Toe" among the Corinthians, at Almack's in the West.*

Almack's was presided over by seven high-born ladies, the 'patronesses', with Lady Jersey in command. This group had the sole right to grant admission vouchers to the subscription balls. Their 'list' never held more than two thousand names, and getting in was a social challenge. The patronesses were autocratic, and those on the list had no choice but to obey their rules. After 11 p.m. no one was admitted – the Duke of Wellington was once turned away at 11.07 p.m. because of lateness and unsuitable attire (he was wearing trousers instead of knee breeches). Formal dress of knee breeches and chapeau-bras (collapsible military hats, meant to be tucked under arms) was de rigueur, and gambling was permitted only at very low stakes. No alcohol was served and the drinks offered included lemonade, orgeat and tea, with stale cake, bread and butter for sustenance, so gentlemen generally found this august establishment insipid and very dull.

The dances were extremely decorous, with a safe distance between couples always strictly maintained. The stately minuet lasted longer at Almack's than at most other places, and old-fashioned quadrilles, cotillions and country dances were the order of the evening. When lively Countess Lieven (one of the patronesses) introduced the waltz to Almack's, this risqué dance, which involved the gentleman putting his arm around his partner's waist, caused a memorable stir.

Admission to Almack's implied acceptance by the ton, which made its balls the most socially desirable in the land. As wit and writer of society verse Henry Luttrell complained:

> If once to Almack's you belong,
> Like monarchs, you can do no wrong;
> But banished thence on Wednesday night,
> By Jove, you can do nothing right.

How Mrs Bennet would have loved the opportunity to shepherd her five girls through the sacred portals of Almack's!

Private balls

*'The proposal of dancing – originating nobody exactly knew where –
was so effectually promoted by Mr and Mrs Cole, that everything
was rapidly clearing away, to give proper space.'*
EMMA

Mr Bingley, planning to host a private ball at Netherfield, sends out his 'cards'. Such invitations usually went out two to three weeks before the event, and those invited were expected to reply within a day or so. It can be safely assumed that a grateful reply was sent from the Bennet house within minutes of the invitation being received. Indeed, all of Meryton would have been sent into fevers of excitement or despair over the arrival or non-arrival of an invitation to the Netherfield ball. For private dances were more prestigious than the public ones to which the vulgar and the lower classes had access. Private balls were 'invitation only', so far more exclusive. In her fiction Jane Austen describes a wonderful range of private balls, from those well planned in advance, to spur-of-the-moment affairs when the carpets were rolled back, the furniture pulled to the walls, and space made for young people to form a set and begin to dance.

Private balls in *Sense and Sensibility*

All the private dances held in *Sense and Sensibility* are at the home of Sir John and Lady Middleton. Jane Austen uses these occasions, which she does not describe in any detail, to illustrate character.

Sir John Middleton is a sportsman, but as he cannot hunt every day of the year, he also gives parties: 'he delighted in collecting about him more young people than his house would hold, and the noisier they were the better was he pleased. He was a blessing to all the juvenile part of the neighbourhood . . . and in winter his private balls were numerous enough for any young lady who was not suffering under the insatiable appetite of fifteen.' Soon after the Dashwoods arrive in Barton the 'private balls at the park then began'. When one party of pleasure is cancelled, Sir John quickly arranges a dance instead. It is not every country squire who would throw his house open to all the locals. Sir John's generosity and kindness to the Dashwood women is in strong contrast to the cold meanness of the relatives they have just left behind at Norland. This John's hospitable parties highlight the parsimony of the novel's other John, John Dashwood.

Jane Austen's main aim, however, in including private dances in this novel is to illustrate the reckless streak in Marianne and the irresponsibility of Willoughby. Both of them love to dance (Willoughby once danced 'at a little hop at the park . . . from eight o'clock till four, with-

Newport Pagnell. Mrs Hurst dancing
Sep.r 17. 1816.

out once sitting down'), but they do not love the rules of the ballroom. These rules stated that a young lady should not stand up for more than two dances in one evening with the same man. If she did so, she was made 'particular' and appeared forward or immodest. Yet this is what Marianne does: 'If dancing formed the amusement of the night, they were partners for half the time; and when obliged to separate for a couple of dances, were careful to stand together and scarcely spoke a word to any body else. Such conduct made them of course most exceedingly laughed at; but ridicule could not shame, and seemed hardly to provoke them.' 'Half the time' means far more than two dances in one evening, and by standing together and talking, they are making themselves conspicuously unavailable to other potential partners. Willoughby is taking risks with Marianne's reputation in a ballroom, so it later comes as no surprise to the reader to learn that he has risked illegitimate pregnancy with another young woman. Marianne can endanger her own reputation by dancing only with Willoughby and thinking nothing of her obligations to her host and hostess or to her Barton community. Later she will endanger her good name by flinging herself at Willoughby at a London party and even risk her life by allowing grief and the neglect of her own health to take her perilously close to suicide.

Dancing is not a major feature of *Sense and Sensibility* but it is used to display the truth of Willoughby's and Marianne's characters, and to foreshadow their future behaviour in the story.

Private balls in *Pride and Prejudice*

Pride and Prejudice contains two very different private dances – one informal and the other formal. The first takes place at an evening party at Sir William Lucas's. Mr Darcy and Mr Bingley are guests and while Bingley spends his time dancing with Jane Bennet, Mr Darcy stands and looks at her sister: 'Occupied in observing Mr Bingley's attentions to her sister, Elizabeth was far from suspecting that she was herself becoming an object of some interest in the eyes of his friend. Mr Darcy had at first scarcely allowed her to be pretty; he had looked at her without admiration at the ball; and when they next met, he looked at her only to criticise. But no sooner had he made it clear to himself and his friends that she had hardly a good feature in her face, than he began to find it was rendered uncommonly intelligent by the beautiful expression of her dark eyes . . . He began to wish to know more of her.'

To achieve this aim, Darcy listens in on Elizabeth's conversation with Colonel Forster – she, showing a decided resemblance to her sister Lydia, is spiritedly teasing the colonel to host a ball at Meryton. Charlotte Lucas then carries her off to play and sing for the company and after Elizabeth's performance, Mary takes over. After tiring everyone with 'a long concerto', Mary was 'glad to purchase praise and gratitude by [playing] Scotch and Irish airs, at the request of her younger sisters, who with some of the Lucases and two or three officers joined eagerly in dancing at one end of the room'. This is a memorable moment in *Pride and Prejudice* because it is the only time Mary Bennet is ever praised or thanked for anything! The reader can easily picture the Lucas drawing room, filled with young people, with the scarlet coats of the officers and tinted muslins of the girls adding colour and grace, the energetic pushing back of furniture to make room for the impromptu dance, and Mary sitting solemnly at the pianoforte.

Mr Darcy, 'in silent indignation at such a mode of passing the evening, to the exclusion of all conversation', stands nearby, until he is approached by the well-meaning and affable Sir William Lucas:

'What a charming amusement for young people this is, Mr Darcy! – There is nothing like dancing after all. – I consider it as one of the first refinements of polished societies.'
'Certainly, Sir; – and it has the advantage also of being in vogue amongst the less polished societies of the world. Every savage can dance.'
Sir William only smiled.

In this scene Jane Austen has brought her hero and heroine together for the second time. The first time they met Darcy was rude and Elizabeth could only suffer his insult in silence, so Darcy emerged from their encounter triumphant. This second time they meet is very different. Once again, we are shown Darcy's tactlessness, this time directed against Sir William Lucas. Darcy's 'Every savage can dance' is a cutting put-down, but Sir William is too polite to respond. He ignores Darcy's aversion to dancing and tries to find him a partner:

> Elizabeth at that instant moving towards them, he was struck with the notion of doing a very gallant thing, and called out to her,
>   'My dear Miss Eliza, why are not you dancing? – Mr Darcy, you must allow me to present this young lady to you as a very desirable partner . . .' And taking her hand, he would have given it to Mr Darcy, who, though extremely surprised, was not unwilling to receive it, when she instantly drew back.

This scene is a brilliant foreshadowing of Darcy's first proposal to Elizabeth halfway through the novel. Sir William's words 'You must allow me . . .' will be echoed when Darcy asks for her hand in marriage ('You must allow me to tell you how ardently I admire and love you.') Darcy 'with grave propriety requested to be allowed the honour of her hand' in the dance, 'but in vain. Elizabeth was determined'. And even though she snubs him, 'Her resistance had not injured her with the gentleman.' She refuses his offer to dance, just as she will refuse his proposal later on. Elizabeth may have come off second-best in her first encounter with Darcy, but she walks off the victor in this, their second.

Jane Austen's most famous private ball is Mr Bingley's Netherfield ball, held in chapter eighteen of *Pride and Prejudice*. It begins as an evening of great expectation for Elizabeth, but she is doomed to disappointment. Instead of dancing with Mr Wickham and achieving 'the conquest of all that remained unsubdued of his heart', she has to dance with bumble-footed and boring Mr Collins, and with silent Mr Darcy. Elizabeth is so cross when she discovers Wickham's absence that she can barely be polite to Darcy who, she believes, is responsible for it. 'But

Elizabeth was not formed for ill-humour; and though every prospect of her own was destroyed for the evening, it could not dwell long on her spirits.' She has a good moan to Charlotte and feels better.

After the misery of two dances with Mr Collins, 'dances of mortification', Elizabeth dances with an officer, and is then invited to dance by Mr Darcy. This time there is no prodding by Sir William, and instead he purposefully approaches her and applies for her hand. This time, Elizabeth is so taken by surprise that she accepts and he leads her on to the floor. This very first dance of hero and heroine is one of Jane Austen's great 'set-pieces' of the novel. The dialogue between them is electric, tension builds, tempers are frayed.

At first Darcy is silent, but Elizabeth will not let him get away with that. She needles him into an argument. Darcy does his best to be agreeable, and his complaisance disconcerts Elizabeth and she can only observe 'that private balls are much pleasanter than public ones' before relapsing into silence herself. In her irritation with the man, she wants battle, but Mr Darcy refuses to fight. Indeed, he takes her hint and resumes conversation when the movements of the dance permit it. And, once again, Elizabeth, unable to resist the temptation, prods him to fight with her. He tries desperately to talk of books before they move to the subject of 'prejudice'. This causes such friction that it brings all conversation to a close and 'they went down the other dance and parted in silence; on each side dissatisfied'. Darcy redirects his dissatisfaction outwards – to Wickham – but Elizabeth's is turned inwards, where it festers and grows until it explodes when Darcy eventually proposes.

The rest of this private ball is misery for Elizabeth. She has to listen to Miss Bingley's sneering interference, undergo the shame of watching Mr Collins's fawning approach to Mr Darcy, endure close confinement with her vulgar mother during supper, and witness Mary's 'exhibiting' at the piano. Mr Collins's sticking by her side prevents her from dancing with other men, and she knows at the end of the night that her family has overstayed its welcome. Little wonder that 'she blushed and blushed again with shame and vexation'.

Elizabeth has little reason to be satisfied with this private ball, but not so her creator. This important ball scene greatly advances Darcy's and Elizabeth's knowledge of each other and increases her attraction in his eyes, but it also makes Darcy aware of Mrs Bennet's hopes for Jane and Bingley's marriage, and so Darcy forms a resolution during this evening of getting his friend away. He does not think Bingley should marry into such a vulgar family and, to do Darcy justice, the Bennets have been particularly inelegant on this night. Darcy's pride is roused against her family, and her prejudice against him is deepened. The Netherfield ball is a rich mix of qualities and emotions – pride, prejudice, vulgarity, shame, resentment, embarrassment and contempt. All those feelings Jane Austen stirs up in her dancing characters add memorably to the developing tension of *Pride and Prejudice*

Private balls in *Mansfield Park*

When the Dashwood and Bennet sisters enter a ballroom, they do so with the confidence that comes from experience. They know the correct etiquette, they are sure of their dance steps, and they have danced their way through cotillions and country dances with a variety of partners. But Fanny Price of *Mansfield Park* lacks this experience and greets with uncertainty the two opportunities she gets to dance within the novel.

As in *Pride and Prejudice*, *Mansfield Park* contains two private dances, again the first an impromptu one, and the second a formal affair. The first takes place just before the group of young people start their theatricals, so they are all in want of amusement. Mr Yates and the Crawfords are in the house and the dance is 'the thought only of the afternoon'. 'It was Fanny's first ball, though without the preparation or splendour of many a young lady's first ball.' For some time it appears that not only is it without splendour, but might also be without any partners for her except Edmund. She sits, 'waiting and wishing' with her two aunts, hoping her cousin Tom will come and ask her to dance. When he appears, he is ungracious: 'He came towards their little circle; but instead of asking her to dance, drew a chair near her, and gave her an account of the present state of a sick horse . . . Fanny found that it was not to be, and in the modesty of her nature immediately felt that she had been unreasonable in expecting it.' Tom does ask her to dance, but in such a way as to make it clear he has no desire to dance with her, and so Fanny refuses. Only to escape playing whist with the older people does he finally lead her to the dance floor.

But while Fanny is sitting, she is watching the dancers, noticing Maria's sparkling animation when Henry Crawford is near her, Julia's pleasure in dancing with Henry, Mrs Grant's willingness to abandon her husband to cards and dance with Mr Yates, though in doing so she deprives an unmarried girl (Fanny) of a partner. The ball is an illustration of selfishness – Tom's selfishness in not thinking of Fanny's pleasure, Maria's in wanting the attention of her sister's dance partner and Mrs Grant's thoughtlessness in depriving Fanny of a partner. The scene closes with Tom railing against the selfishness of his Aunt Norris, totally unaware that he is describing himself as well as her as he rants: 'And to ask me in such a way too! without ceremony, before them all, so as to leave me no possibility of refusing! . . . If I had not luckily thought of standing up with you I could not have got out of it. It is a great deal too bad.' In contrast to all this egoism is Fanny's youthful, happy enjoyment of her first little ball.

Fanny at her first dance is so modest that she feels she is presumptuous to expect Tom to dance with her at all. She certainly feels, in the next volume of *Mansfield Park*, that she is not entitled to have a ball held in her honour. It frightens her that her uncle has it all arranged: 'Sir Thomas had been amusing himself with shaping a very complete outline of the business; and as soon as [Mrs Norris] would listen quietly, could read his list of the families to be invited, from whom he calculated, with all necessary allowance for the shortness of the notice, to collect young people enough to form twelve or fourteen couple.' He sends out his invitation cards and makes many a young lady happy by doing so, but not his niece: 'To her, the cares were sometimes almost beyond the happiness'. She doesn't know what to wear or how to hang her amber cross, and she worries about Edmund dancing with Mary and so fails to have 'half the enjoyment in anticipation which she ought to have had.' Fanny does not want to be 'Queen of the evening'; she desires

only to 'dance without much observation or any extraordinary fatigue', and to dance with Edmund.

Fanny's ball is given for display. Sir Thomas wants to show her off as a suitable wife for Henry Crawford. He wants Henry to see Fanny against the wealth and status of *Mansfield Park*, to be made fully aware of her grand connections. What better way to do so than to light up one's ballroom and give all the neighbours a feast of food and wine! To have Fanny behave like a shrinking violet is therefore contrary to his purpose. She must be properly dressed by his wife's maid (though that doesn't eventuate), open the ball, and be sent to bed when her looks supposedly fade due to weariness. She must be introduced to the local gentry (and what a telling sign it is of her sheltered life thus far that Fanny doesn't even know the neighbours!) and she must be carefully watched during the evening.

In spite of nerves and confusions, Fanny enjoys her first formal ball: 'Fanny had a good deal of enjoyment in the course of the evening . . . She was happy whenever she looked at William, and saw how perfectly he was enjoying himself . . . she was happy in having the two dances with Edmund.' Once again Jane Austen depicts Fanny's happiness as a contrast to the selfishness of the others. Sir Thomas looks on Fanny with pleasure only because she reflects back to him his own status and wealth. Edmund cannot rouse himself from depression over Mary to be a cheerful dance partner to Fanny: 'I have been talking incessantly all night, and with nothing to say, But with you, Fanny, there may be peace. You will not want to be talked to.' Mrs Norris is unhappy because she egotistically wanted to organize it all and her instructions are being ignored. At the end of the night, Sir Thomas selfishly uses his 'absolute power' and sends Fanny to bed. This is an unusual occurrence – a young lady for whom the ball is being given normally remained visible to the guests for as long as the ball lasted. Tiredness and lack of energy were not usually desirable qualities to prospective partners. But Sir Thomas, as well as indulgently wishing to exert his own power, wants to demonstrate to Henry Crawford that Fanny is biddable and obedient, that she has sensibility and needs dominant men to tell her what to do – all qualities which do seem to prove attractive to Henry Crawford, for he is even more enamoured of Fanny by the end of the night. Fanny is tired, but would have rather just sat and watched than gone to bed. However, she obeys, stopping at the door to look back on 'five or six determined couple, who were still hard at work', and 'feeling, in spite of everything, that a ball was indeed delightful'.

Pride and Prejudice used dancing to further the romance of hero and heroine. There dancing was about courtship, verbal sparring, misunderstandings between Darcy and Elizabeth. *Mansfield Park* employs dance very differently. Dance does nothing in this book to make Fanny and Edmund more in love or better acquainted. Some dancing takes place off stage – for example, Maria and Mr Rushworth are engaged after 'dancing with each other at a proper number of balls'. But when dancing occurs within the novel, it is there thematically, displaying selfish pride and power, self-absorption, and selfish competition. Not a word is wasted in this brilliant novel, and nor is a single dance step.

Private balls in *Emma*

Remaining with her pattern of one informal private dance, followed by one formal one, Jane Austen uses dance in *Emma* to reveal the true state of her heroine's heart. Both these dances are depicted through Emma's consciousness – we share her anxieties and hopes and view the assembled company through her eyes.

The evening at the Coles is not planned as a ball. Mr and Mrs Cole invite their neighbours to dine with them, with 'less worthy females' adding to the numbers after dinner. Then there are musical performances from Emma and Jane Fairfax and it is only at the very end of the evening that a 'proposal of dancing – originating nobody exactly knew where' is made. Jane Austen gives no further clues as to who the originator is, but as it is totally in keeping with Frank's character that he would want to dance with Jane, it is not hard to work out that he is the guilty party. Mrs Weston sits down to the piano, and Frank dutifully asks Emma to dance (all as part of his cover for his true relationship with Jane) and leads her 'up to the top' of the set.

Frank might be Emma's partner, but he does not have her attention. Her recent conversation with Mrs Weston over the possibility of Mr Knightley being in love with Jane has alarmed Emma: 'While waiting till the other young people could pair themselves off, Emma found time . . . to look about, and see what became of Mr Knightley. This would be a trial. He was no dancer in general. If he were to be very alert in engaging Jane Fairfax now, it might augur something. There was no immediate appearance. No; he was talking to Mrs Cole – he was looking on unconcerned; Jane was asked by somebody else, and he was still talking to Mrs Cole.' Emma is able to relax and lead off the dance 'with genuine spirit and enjoyment'. Had Mr Knightley been leading Jane Fairfax into the set, Emma's happiness in the dance would have been destroyed. In this novel so full of 'clues', Jane Austen here provides an important indication of the true state of Emma's emotions – she might dance with Frank Churchill, but her eyes and thoughts are with Mr Knightley.

And Frank is equally distracted. 'Two dances, unfortunately, were all that could be allowed. It was growing late . . . After some attempts, therefore, to be permitted to begin again, they were obliged to . . . look sorrowful, and have done.' Frank has lost his chance to dance with Jane – he clearly tries to keep the dancing going just a bit longer, but can in the end only hide his disappointment (and reveal the direction of his thoughts) by saying to Emma: 'Perhaps it is as well . . . I must have asked Miss Fairfax, and her languid dancing would not have agreed with me, after your's.'

No private ball in Jane Austen's novels is as planned, postponed and discussed as the ball held at the Crown Inn by the Westons. It takes place in an inn, which technically makes it a public rather than a private ball, but it is definitely 'invitation only' and is hosted and paid for by

the Westons for the private enjoyment of themselves and their friends.
Frank Churchill, deprived of his dance with Jane, is determined to try
again: He 'had danced once at Highbury, and longed to dance again;
and the last half hour of an evening
which Mr Woodhouse was persuaded
to spend with his daughter at Randalls,
was passed by the two young people in
schemes on the subject. Frank's was the
first idea; and his the greatest zeal in pur-
suing it.' Rooms are measured, numbers
are calculated, but the Westons' home
will not do. Even then Frank is undaunt-
ed, and plans are made to hold it at the
Crown Inn instead. Frank hurries off to
get Miss Bates and her niece to come
and help 'do away difficulties'.

> '. . . when a beginning is made – when the felicities of rapid motion have once been, though slightly, felt – it must be a very heavy set that does not ask for more.' *Emma*

The ball is postponed and Emma is
wretched at 'the loss of the ball'. 'Such a delightful evening as it would
have been! – Every body so happy!' Jane Fairfax is even more disappointed and actually falls sick. Before too long, the ball scheme is revived and a
day fixed. 'Mr Weston's ball was to be a real thing. A very few tomorrows
stood between the young people of Highbury and happiness.'

It proves to be an eventful ball and much is achieved by Jane Aus-
ten both on and off the dance floor. Numerous clues are dropped as to
Frank's real romantic interest – he is restlessly on the lookout for Miss
Bates and then keeps looking at Jane when she arrives. The hopes of the
Westons are shown to lie in another direction – they are pleased when
Frank opens the ball with Emma. The Eltons are rude to Harriet and
Mr Knightley once again displays his true gentility by rescuing Harriet
from embarrassment, thus making the girl fall in love with him. Miss
Bates's long speeches give away much information as to Jane's depres-
sion, what is served for supper and who has been invited.

However, it is through Emma's watchful eyes that we see most of
the Crown Inn ball. Her disappointment over not opening the ball and

being forced to take second place to Mrs Elton dents her happiness to begin with. But an even greater source of disquiet comes from seeing that Mr Knightley is not dancing. Once again, although partnered by Frank, Emma looks first for Mr Knightley: 'There he was, among the standers-by, where he ought not to be; he ought to be dancing, – not classing himself with the husbands, and fathers, and whist-players, who were pretending to feel an interest in the dance till their rubbers were made up, – so young as he looked! – He could not have appeared to greater advantage perhaps any where, than where he had placed himself. His tall, firm, upright figure, among the bulky forms and stooping shoulders of the elderly men, was such as Emma felt must draw every body's eyes; and, excepting her own partner, there was not one among the whole row of young men who could be compared with him. – He moved a few steps nearer, and those few steps were enough to prove in how gentlemanlike a manner, with what natural grace, he must have danced, would he but take the trouble. – Whenever she caught his eye, she forced him to smile; but in general he was looking grave. She wished he could love a ball-room better, and could like Frank Churchill better. – He seemed often observing her.' That means that Emma is observing him too, wanting him to smile at her, thinking about him and worrying about him.

Dancing, as Henry Tilney has pointed out, is emblematic of courtship and marriage. The very language is the same – making 'an offer of a hand', 'engaging' for a dance or making a 'proposal' to dance. What disturbs Emma is that Mr Knightley has withdrawn himself from this activity, has placed himself with the married men and confirmed bachelors at the side of the room. His apparent lack of availability to her as a dance/marriage partner makes her suddenly aware of his youth and desirability. 'Tall, firm, upright' are tempting terms going through Emma's mind, and as she moves about the dance floor, her eyes are perpetually drawn back to this newly attractive Mr Knightley. David Selwyn writes perceptively of this scene in his chapter on 'Dancing' in *Jane Austen and Leisure*: 'There is no comment on Emma's dancing, or on Frank Churchill's: the graceful movement is made by the man who is not dancing, and

Among the bulky forms and stooping shoulders

it is allied to moral qualities of the gentlemanly and the natural.' Emma is puzzled by his gravity and fails to realize it is caused by jealousy as he watches her dance with Frank. They speak no words, but so much is conveyed, and misconveyed, through the language of their eyes.

The evening is a busy one for Emma. She still finds time to note that Mr Knightley's dancing 'proved to be just what she had believed it, extremely good' and to envy Harriet for her happiness in being his partner. As soon as she has a free moment, 'her eyes invited [Mr Knightley] irresistibly to come to her'. They share a frank and generous conversation about the Eltons' rudeness, but are interrupted by Mr Weston 'calling on every body to begin dancing again': 'Whom are you going to dance with?' Mr Knightley asks Emma. There is a moment's hesitation. A young lady had to wait to be asked and not do the asking herself (just as in a marriage proposal). But Emma's slowly awakening consciousness of Mr Knightley's allure and her determination that he must not be classed as an old bachelor make her brave: 'With you, if you will ask me', she replies, and Mr Knightley does ask and offers her his hand. Subconsciously anxious that nothing stand in the way of her love for Mr Knightley, Emma does away with another possible impediment to their love: 'You know we are not really so much brother and sister as to make it at all improper.' Mr Knightley, far more aware of his true feelings than Emma is of hers, responds emphatically, 'Brother and sister! no, indeed.'

Brothers and sisters could, and often did, dance with each other (Fanny and William Price are an example) and there was nothing improper about it. But this was only when they were children, for of course brothers and sisters do not look at each other romantically and should not be placed in any position where such looks were virtually expected (Fanny and William Price do not dance together, as adults, at the Mansfield ball). Emma and Mr Knightley are only brother-in-law and sister-in-law but Emma wants it made quite plain that they do not view each other as close relations. She does not know why she wants this point cleared up, but it is strangely important to her that it is. Mr Knightley most definitely agrees. The ball at the Crown Inn marks the beginning of a move from their family relationship to a romantic one.

Private balls in *Persuasion*

One of Jane Austen's saddest scenes depicts Anne Elliot of *Persuasion* sitting at the piano playing dance tunes while her eyes fill with tears. As with the dinner at the Coles' in *Emma*, this dinner party at the Musgroves has closed unexpectedly: 'The evening ended with dancing. On its being proposed, Anne offered her services, as usual; and though her eyes would sometimes fill with tears as she sat at the instrument, she was extremely glad to be employed, and desired nothing in return but to be unobserved.'

This is not the first time Anne's musical services have been required. The Musgrove girls are 'wild for dancing' and when their Hayter cousins visit, Anne plays by the hour for their 'unpremeditated little ball[s]' and earns the praise and gratitude of Mr and Mrs Musgrove by doing so. As there is no one Anne wants to dance with, she is happy to be useful and busy.

But then Captain Wentworth comes back into her life, and memories of their courtship (which must have included dancing with each other) and their broken engagement return to pain her. As she plays, she watches Henrietta and Louisa flirt with him, the young Miss Hayters fall for him, and everyone except her is having fun. It is not selfishness that makes Anne cry – Anne Elliot is never selfish – but deep regret and a broken heart. She does not even manage to gain her wish of remaining unnoticed: 'Once she felt that he was looking at herself – observing her altered features, perhaps trying to trace in them the ruins of the face which had once charmed him; and once she knew that he must have spoken of her; – she was hardly aware of it till she heard the answer; but then she was sure of his having asked his partner whether Miss Elliot never danced? The answer was, "Oh! no, never; she has quite given up

> 'There was a family of cousins within a walk of Uppercross . . . they would come at any time, and help play at any thing, or dance any where; and Anne . . . played country dances to them by the hour together.'
> *Persuasion*

dancing."'

Sadly it appears that statement is correct and that Anne's dancing
days are over, for Jane Austen never shows her dancing. The fact that
she is considered to have willingly given up indicates how much Anne is
regarded as a confirmed old maid by all around her. Only Lady Russell
(not present in this Uppercross scene) ever thinks that Anne still has
chances of marriage. Anne does not try to change this general percep-
tion of her spinsterhood – indeed, she reinforces it by taking the office
of musician so entirely upon herself. Here, dancing is a metaphor for
happiness and romance, so there is a haunting sadness in this vignette
of Anne weeping at the piano while others dance joyfully around her.
Readers can only hope that when Captain Wentworth marries her and
they embark on 'their settled life' she will be able, once again, to dance
with the man she adores.

Jane Austen attends private balls

The Austens were not a rich family, but occasionally Jane Austen attended some very exclusive private balls. Local aristocrats, the Earl and
Countess of Portsmouth, gave a ball in November 1800, to which she
was invited. She found it 'a pleasant evening' and, as she danced only
nine dances out of the twelve, had time to look about her: 'there were
very few Beauties, & such as there were, were not very handsome'. She
enjoyed noting the broad faces and fat necks, bad breath, ugly husbands and energetic dancers. Perhaps the Portsmouths felt they had
been too generous to their guests, for the next year Jane's friend Mrs
Lefroy reported to her that a tiny supper was served with bad wine. The
Dorchesters of Kempshott Park hosted an annual ball for the benefit of
their own large family and all their Hampshire neighbours. Jane Austen
danced at Kempshott in 1799, and managed to procure an invitation for
her brother Charles so that he could share in the treat (but Charles in
the end could not attend).

Less grand for her were the private balls hosted by local squires. The
Bramstons of Oakley Hall, the Harwoods of Deane, the Wildmans of
Chilham, the Bigg-Withers of Manydown and the Lefroys of Ashe Rec-

tory, all gave balls attended by Jane Austen and her family. Such events must have been great fun for her. She was with people she had known all her life – the Terrys, Digweeds, Warrens, Catherine and Alethea Bigg, the Chutes, and others with whom she could laugh and flirt, stay the night and talk it all over the next day. Her first surviving letter describes a ball at Manydown in just such company: 'I danced twice with Warren last night', she reported to Cassandra, 'and once with Mr Charles Watkins, and, to my inexpressible astonishment, I entirely escaped John Lyford. I was forced to fight hard for it, however. We had a very good supper, and the greenhouse was illuminated in a very elegant manner.' These private balls may not have been held in the stately homes of the neighbourhood, but she probably gained far more enjoyment from them.

Courtship, avoidance, getting tipsy, remaining without a partner, and amusedly watching the company to see who misbehaved and who did not – Jane Austen experienced it all at private dances. When she sat down at her desk to depict her characters dancing in each other's homes, she had a wealth of experience to draw on.

Ashe Rectory, where Jane Austen often danced with family and friends.

Court balls

Court balls were the social pinnacle of all private balls and Mrs Bennet, Mrs Elton and Miss Thorpe would have given their eye teeth to be invited to one. These prestigious events were held at the royal palace of St James's and were usually to celebrate a royal birthday. In 1818 a very splendid ball was held in honour of Queen Charlotte's birthday. All the members of the royal family made an appearance and were welcomed with military honours and salutes, foreign ambassadors and their wives were presented to their majesties, and the Lord Chancellor, Lord Mayor and other civic dignitaries also bowed to their majesties and danced at the ball. So that nothing should mar the beauty and happiness of the occasion, mourning was put off for the day by those who had recently suffered a death in the family. Only bright colours were considered suitable for a royal ball.

During the reign of George III, most court balls were held at St James's, but music and dancing were sometimes offered at Buckingham House (purchased by the King for his wife in 1762). Sir William Lucas, when mayor of a town near Meryton, was presented at the court of St James, but whether he danced while there is not stated in the novel. He would certainly have been aware, however, of the status of court balls and he tries to flatter Mr Darcy by suggesting to him, 'Do you not think it would be a proper compliment to the place?' Many young men would have, like Mr Darcy, avoided these court balls. They were stuffy, excessively formal affairs – not much fun for a red-blooded young man. The Prince Regent regularly got drunk at those given in honour of his parents.

> '"Do you often dance at St James's?" Sir William Lucas asks Mr Darcy. But no, Mr Darcy never does and, he makes it clear to Sir William, he has no desire to.'
>
> *Pride and Prejudice*

"Come, Darcy," said he,
"I must have you dance."

Etiquette of the ballroom

'One of the first refinements of polished societies'
PRIDE AND PREJUDICE

The rules and regulations of the ballrooms of Jane Austen's day dated back, in the main, to the time of Beau Nash, arbiter of good behaviour in public places, who wrote *Rules to be Observ'd at Bath* in 1706.

One should never attend a private ball without an invitation.
In *Catharine, or The Bower*, Edward Stanley follows his family to a ball given by Mr and Mrs Dudley, without any invitation. When Catharine raises some scruples, he replies, 'Oh! hang them; who cares for that; they cannot turn me out of the house.' But the Dudleys do care, feel 'their dignity injured', and treat him with great haughtiness. Elizabeth Bennet wonders if Wickham has not come to Mr Bingley's ball because he has not received an invitation, but is assured that all the officers were invited. Jane Austen was often at some pains to procure invitations for her brothers. Even when these balls were hosted by good friends and neighbours, she never took the liberty of bringing along her brothers Charles or Frank if no invitation had been issued.

A gentleman could not ask a lady to dance unless they had been formally introduced.
Henry Tilney needs master of ceremonies Mr King to introduce him to Catherine Morland before he can ask her to dance. Mr Bingley, eager to be introduced to Jane Bennet so that he can dance with her, 'asks to be introduced'. Any stranger could be

introduced to a partner after applying to the master of ceremonies, so it was usually easy to gain introductions – Elizabeth chides Darcy by telling him satirically, 'True; and nobody can ever be introduced in a ball room.' However, you did need to know someone, or find the MC, in order to bring an introduction about, and in Bath Mrs Allen knows not a soul, so Catherine Morland must remain without partners the entire night.

A lady must accept an invitation to dance, or spend the rest of the evening sitting out all the dances (unless she was seriously tired).

Elizabeth Bennet had hoped to reserve the opening dances at the Netherfield ball for Mr Wickham, so is most put out when Mr Collins asks her to save them for him. However, she is obliged to accept his offer if she wants to dance with anyone else during that first set. And if Mr Collins continues to stand by her the entire evening, other men are not likely to ask her to dance. By the end of the night, Elizabeth decides that she would rather remain without any partner at all than undergo the misery of another dance with Mr Collins.

A couple could dance a maximum of two sets (i.e. two pairs of dances) with each other. After that, they were expected to do their social duty and find other partners.

Dancing was a community activity, so if a couple danced exclusively with each other, they were neglecting their duties as members of that community. Marianne and Willoughby break this rule – 'they were partners for half the time'; and so do Isabella Thorpe and James Morland. Isabella protests that it is 'quite shocking' and puts the blame on James, but she knows she is behaving badly. Catharine, of *Catharine, or The Bower*, dances 'during the greatest part' of the evening with Mr Stanley, but as she has little experience of balls, she does so from ignorance and not a deliberate flouting of the rules.

A gentleman, single or married, was expected to invite ladies who were available to dance.

Mr Elton blatantly rejects this rule when he sees Harriet Smith without a partner. Even when Mrs Weston points out Harriet's single state, Mr Elton still refuses to dance with her. Other offenders are Lord Osborne, John Thorpe, Tom Bertram with his cousin Fanny, Captain Tilney (unless a very pretty girl catches his eye) and, most memorably, Mr Darcy at the Meryton assembly. By contrast, Mr Knightley well knows this etiquette requirement and shows his true gentility by going to the rescue of Harriet Smith.

Everybody must submit to the decrees of the master of ceremonies.

Thomas Wilson complained that young men at assembly balls were too apt to ignore the master of ceremonies, 'whose authority is unquestionable, and decisions final'. He called him the 'Arbiter Elegantiarum', and insisted that dancers should submit on all occasions to his behests.

At the end of the dance, the man was expected to usher his partner back to her chaperone, or escort her to the supper room. There they would sit with her family or friends, and not with his.

Henry Tilney obeys this rule when he leads Catherine back to Mrs Allen and then sits with the two ladies discussing muslins. Young Charles Blake is still learning his dance etiquette, so Emma Watson has to gently instruct him. When he suggests they go and sit with the Osborne party for supper, she replies, 'No, no . . . you must sit with my friends.'

A gentleman was expected to be prompt when coming to claim his partner for a dance for which he had previously engaged her.

John Thorpe has reserved a dance with Catherine and then is late arriving to dance it with her. This puts her into the embarrassing position of appearing to be partnerless, yet having to refuse any other man who comes to ask for her hand.

One must dance neatly – do not caper, kick out, bump into others or draw attention to one's dancing in any obvious way.

The younger Bennet girls have yet to learn this rule – they are too noisy, energetic, and frolicsome on the dance floor. There is little hope that Mr Collins will ever learn it – he will remain a terrible dancer, drawing attention to himself because of all his mistakes until the day he dies. Surely Charlotte will make sure that, once married, he never dances again.

Couples had to join longways country dance sets from the bottom, and not race up to the top or push in between other couples.

In *Catharine, or The Bower*, the heroine is hurried by Edward Stanley to the top of the set. This behaviour is 'highly resented by several young Ladies present' as neither she nor her partner have the rank to justify taking first place in the set. Nor have they drawn tickets in a lottery to entitle them to this elevated position. Catharine is given little choice, but Edward Stanley should have known better.

It was bad form to save too many dances in advance and leave no room on one's dance programme for requests on the night.

Marianne and Willoughby are the worst offenders here. They determine well before any dance that they will dance almost exclusively with each other. Country dancers of today still regard such behaviour as highly ill-mannered.

Paying compliments on one's partner's appearance was not done. It was assumed that everybody would be appropriately dressed, and that a dressmaker or tailor did not need to be praised for doing their job properly.

Mrs Elton, so distressed at receiving no compliments on her gown and jewellery from her partner Mr Weston, takes the task upon herself and reveals her vulgarity when she loudly forces Jane

Fairfax to make compliments on her gown and appearance. Miss Bates knows this and although she looks at Emma with great admiration, she says, 'Must not compliment, I know . . . that would be rude.'

Gloves must be worn by both sexes at all times, except at supper.
Frank Churchill buys new gloves when he arrives in Highbury in the hope that they will be used if he gets an opportunity to dance with Jane Fairfax.

Gentlemen, officers on duty excepted, will not be given entry if wearing boots.
Captain Denny and the other officers quartered in Meryton would have all danced at Meryton in their shiny Hessians, as would Captain Tilney in the public rooms in Bath, but Edmund Bertram, Mr Knightley and other non-military men would never have dreamed of wearing boots in a ballroom, and would have donned evening shoes instead.

Respect other people at all times.
Balls were an opportunity for display of all sorts – of your person, your status, your importance in the community – but such display was expected to be discreet. Balls were the most important social events of the day, and it was critical that everyone had a good time. If some were pushy, rude, noisy, or generally inconsiderate, then everyone suffered as a result. Jane Austen shows many examples of people breaking the above rules, and the consequences are discussed within the community and can damage the reputations of the offenders. Balls, in her novels, reveal true gentility, contrast good manners with bad ones, and show that fun can be had by all, if only everyone behaves.

Opening a ball

Which lucky young lady opened the assembly ball held at Meryton at the start of *Pride and Prejudice*? Mrs Bennet, listing all Mr Bingley's dances to her husband when she gets home, unfortunately fails to tell us. It could have been any of the young women present. As the Bennet girls filed through the door of the assembly rooms they could 'draw for numbers'. This process of ticket taking gave each of them a chance to 'open the ball', which involved dancing at the head of the first set at the top of the room, and also being invited to choose which sort of dance would be played. The master of ceremonies would then call out the numbers and assign all the ladies and their partners to places.

However, had a lady of distinguished rank been there, she would have opened the ball instead. The etiquette connected with that first dance was rather complicated and must have often led to rather unseemly jostling for position, and to frequent offence being given. In *The Watsons* the honour would have fallen to Miss Osborne of Osborne Castle, as the lady of highest rank, but she only arrives after the ball has started. The master of ceremonies would have had to decide whether to issue tickets or to assume that if the Osbornes came at all, they would arrive late.

At a private ball it was somewhat simpler to sort out who was entitled to open proceedings. Elizabeth Elliot in *Persuasion*, only too aware of her status as eldest daughter of a baronet, opens 'every ball of credit' within the neighbourhood of Kellynch for 'thirteen winters'. It would take a very brave young lady to try to take that honour away from the formidable Miss Elliot, though had she been attending a ball with the Honourable Miss Carteret, she would have been forced to take second place. Emma Woodhouse takes the place of honour for granted when she is 'led up to the top' at the Coles' informal dance.

Bridal status also conferred the right to open a ball. Emma Woodhouse, convinced the Westons are giving their ball especially for her and used to leading the way, forgets

Conducted

he room.

this, as do the Westons: 'It had just occurred to Mrs Weston that Mrs Elton must be asked to begin the ball; that she would expect it; which interfered with all their wishes of giving Emma that distinction. – Emma heard the sad truth with fortitude . . . [she] must submit to stand second to Mrs Elton, though she had always considered the ball as peculiarly for her. It was almost enough to make her think of marrying.' But Mrs Elton, all too aware of her rights as a bride, has not forgotten and is expecting to be asked to open the ball with Frank Churchill.

Traditionally debutantes who were 'coming out' were also assumed to lead the way. This comes as bad news to Fanny Price in *Mansfield Park*: 'Mr Crawford was not far off; Sir Thomas brought him to her, saying something which discovered to Fanny, that she was to lead the way and open the ball; an idea that had never occurred to her before. Whenever she had thought on the minutiae of the evening, it had been as a matter of course that Edmund would begin with Miss Crawford.' Fanny begs Sir Thomas to excuse her, but he insists. 'She could hardly believe it. To be placed above so many elegant young women! The distinction was too great. It was treating her like her cousins!' Fanny is terrified by her leading role: 'she was a great deal too frightened to have any enjoyment, till she could suppose herself no longer looked at'.

Opening a ball gave a young woman the ultimate opportunity for display, and it announced her prestige and her availability on the marriage market. Miss Bingley, Isabella Thorpe, Elizabeth Elliot, and Lucy Steele would all have jumped at the chance. Some grew quite resentful when not given the opportunity, such as Camilla Stanley in *Catharine, or The Bower*: 'I am sure I am not at all offended, and should not care if all the World were to stand above me, but still it is extremely abominable, and what I cannot put up with.' More retiring and modest women such as Fanny, Georgiana Darcy, Anne de Bourgh and Anne Elliot do not relish the public glare that an 'opening' couple were exposed to.

Men in the ballroom

'There was a scarcity of Men in general'
Letter from Jane Austen, 1800

Dancing with officers

When a Regency girl walked into a ballroom, her eye was very likely to be drawn to an officer. Scarlet coats attracted the female gaze as candles attracted a moth, and the bright jacket, tight trousers, gleaming Hessian boots and upright military stance usually proved irresistible to women. Lydia and Kitty Bennet can take no pleasure 'from the society of a man in any other colour' than scarlet, while their mother who, in her youth, 'cried for two days together' when the local regiment left town, still has a partiality for any man in red ('I thought Colonel Forster looked very becoming the other night at Sir William's in his regimentals'). Mrs Bennet would happily give any of her daughters in marriage to 'a smart young Colonel, with five or six thousand a year'. Regiments often selected recruits for their good looks and their height, so army officers usually stood out on a crowded dance floor. In *The Post-Captain*, an 1806 novel by John Davis, the author complains that 'women, like mackerel . . . are caught with a red bait . . . the blue jackets stand no chance'. Mary Edwards in *The Watsons* also likes officers—she begins and ends the assembly ball dancing with Captain Hunter, and is 'surrounded by red coats the whole evening'. Even snooty Miss Osborne from the castle is far from immune to the charms of a scarlet coat; she breaks her promise to dance with young Charles Blake to stand up with a Colonel Beresford. Emma Watson also dances with men in regimentals that evening. Poor Catharine of *Catharine, or The Bower* is 'sometimes obliged to relinquish a Ball because an Officer was to be there', such is her aunt's fear that she may be seduced by his red coat. There was a strong belief that crimson coats totally deranged female minds.

With a militia regiment actually quartered in Meryton for the winter, it is inevitable that the Bennet girls will meet soldiers. Kitty and Lydia can 'talk of nothing but officers' and wish only to dance with men in red coats when they go to balls. Even their clever sister Elizabeth bemoans the absence of Mr Wickham in his smart uniform when she enters the ballroom at Netherfield. Lydia's idea of heaven is a Brighton ballroom filled with officers, all flirting with her. Even in the midst of eloping, Lydia thinks of balls and regimental dance partners: 'Pray make my excuses to Pratt, for not keeping my engagement, and dancing with him tonight', she instructs her friend Mrs Forster. At the end of the novel she becomes a soldier's wife, and Jane Austen describes the Wickhams as always on the move and always in debt. Lydia's dancing days appear to end with her marriage—it is a depressing picture of the disadvantages of succumbing to the lure of a crimson coat at a ball.

> 'But if these soldiers are quicker than other people in a ball room, what are young ladies to do?' *The Watsons*

Marianne Dashwood of *Sense and Sensibility* also becomes the wife of a military man, but he is retired (so has no dashing uniform to attract her) and therefore she is not expected to lead the unsettled life of an army spouse. Nor is she ever depicted dancing with him—indeed, for much of the novel, she thinks he is far too old for dancing. Isabella Thorpe of *Northanger Abbey* hopes to dance herself into the position of wife to an army captain. Frederick Tilney states publicly that he 'hates dancing', and Isabella declares that with her fiancé, James Morland, away in the country, 'she would not dance upon any account in the world', yet these two end up giving 'hands across' as dance partners at a Bath assembly ball. Afterwards she tries to explain her behaviour to her friend Catherine: 'Oh! my dear! It would have looked so particular; and you know how I abhor doing that. I refused him as long as I possibly could,

but he would take no denial. You have no idea how he pressed me.' Flattered and excited, Isabella fails to see that Captain Tilney is merely idly passing time with her and keeping his flirting skills up to date, but Henry Tilney knows his brother is not serious in intention. Of course Isabella is captivated not only by Captain Tilney's scarlet coat, but also by his future fortune as an eldest son – she would exchange poor clergyman James Morland for the rich captain without a moment's hesitation. She is never given the chance, for neither man wants to marry her in the end. It would only add to her bitterness to know that 'the mess-room will drink Isabella Thorpe for a fortnight' and laugh at her frustrated hopes of being an army wife. In an earlier generation of that novel Miss Drummond must have also loved the sight of a red coat, for she married General Tilney, and lived to regret it.

Naval men were not so conspicuous in a ballroom. During the Napoleonic Wars, sailors were more likely to be away at sea, whereas militia regiments were stationed in coastal towns ready and waiting to defend England's shores if the need arose. Army men had little to do, and quickly became part of local society, attending balls, dancing at private parties, and flirting with local girls. When the men of the Royal Navy did spend time on shore, they did not attract the same notice in a ball-room, as they could not wear their uniforms. In fact, William Price of *Mansfield Park* deeply regrets that 'cruel custom prohibited its appearance except on duty'. Even without uniforms, however, the young ladies of Portsmouth seem well aware of the rankings of possible partners. William complains to his sister: 'And I do not know that there would be any good in going to the Assembly, for I might not get a partner. The Portsmouth girls turn up their noses at any body who has not a commission. One might as well be nothing as a midshipman.' Frederick Wentworth, as a naval captain, does not have this problem and finds the Musgrove girls only too eager to dance with him at Uppercross. Generally, however, it was military men rather than the men of the navy who carried the day in the ballroom.

Jane Austen dances with officers

At a ball in 1799, Jane Austen took the eye of a young army officer and reported his interest to her sister in her own inimical style: 'There was one Gentleman, an officer of the Cheshire, a very good look-ing young Man, who I was told wanted very much to be introduced to me; – but as he did not want it quite enough to take much trouble in effecting it, We never could bring it about.' Had the young man bestirred himself a little more, perhaps Jane Austen could have ended up an army wife.

Basingstoke Assembly Rooms, where Jane Austen often danced with officers in her youth.

There were many men in uniform at the balls she attended – she regularly mentions officers by name – and she acknowledged the powers of a red coat over the female mind. Writing to her sister after a Southampton ball, Jane remarked that a mutual acquaintance was happy in having 'an officer to flirt with'. On another occasion she teased her sister about dancing with a Mr Kemble: 'Why did you dance four dances with so stupid a Man? – why not rather dance two of them with some elegant brother-officer who was struck with your appearance as soon as you entered the room?' Both sisters recognized that a fetching uniform could attract quickly. However, there's no doubt that Jane herself preferred naval men to army men, both on the dance floor and in other social settings. With two brothers in the navy, she must often have met their naval colleagues, but there are no special mentions in letters of her dancing with any of them. In her music books she changed the title of the song 'A Soldier's Adieu' to 'A Sailor's Adieu'. The woman who could make such a change was not likely to fall in love with a dance partner in brilliant red.

The shortage of male dance partners

At the Meryton assembly Elizabeth Bennet is 'obliged, by the scarcity of gentlemen, to sit down for two dances'. It is while she is sitting down that Mr Bingley tries to persuade Mr Darcy to dance and even suggests that he ask Elizabeth. Unfortunately, Elizabeth hears Darcy's reply: 'She is tolerable; but not handsome enough to tempt me; and I am in no humour at present to give consequence to young ladies who are slighted by other men.' And so Elizabeth's pride is wounded and her prejudice against Darcy is formed.

Yet Elizabeth's plight was a common one. Many a young lady had to sit out dances, waiting near the chaperones and trying to look as if she didn't care, in the hope that a man would come and ask for the next dance. Some girls were simply plain and did not attract partners. The novelist Mary Russell Mitford was realistic about her chances of a partner at balls: 'What, indeed, should I do at a dance with my dumpling of a person tumbling about like a cricket-ball on uneven ground, or a bowl rolling among nine-pins – casting off with the grace of a frisky Yorkshire cow, or going down the middle with the majesty of an overloaded hay-waggon passing down a narrow lane?' This is also a problem for Charlotte Lucas, Mary Bennet, Anne Steele and the other less eyecatching females of Jane Austen's fiction.

But the major problem was a real shortage of men. During most of Jane Austen's life her country was at war with

France. This war ate up young men – the army took about 100,000 of them, the navy another 130,000. While some of these men were posted in Brighton with nothing to do but flirt with Lydia Bennet, as does George Wickham, others did not have it so easy. Many were killed, or spent hard months in Europe fighting the Peninsular War, or served years away at sea. Some, like two of Jane Austen's brothers, found women living overseas to be their wives. Then there was the overseas expansion of the British Empire, which was also starting to lure young men away – they went as soldiers, missionaries, builders and professional men. Jane's own uncle by marriage, Tysoe Saul Hancock, set off for India to try to make his fortune there. While the occasional boatload of intrepid women followed them to become their brides, most women were not yet travelling to foreign lands. More would move abroad as nurses, teachers, and governesses from about the time of Jane Austen's death. During the Georgian era more baby boys died at birth than baby girls, and of course there were some men who could never afford to marry. By the middle of the nineteenth century, the imbalance between the sexes had reached serious proportions. Britain in 1851 had a surplus of 365,000 women over men. Little wonder that when Jane Austen entered a ballroom she should see more dresses than pantaloons; little wonder that even pretty Elizabeth Bennet should sometimes be partnerless.

Before setting off for the ball, the Bennets fear the situation could be even worse. Mr Bingley has left town for a few days – will he be back in time for the ball, so that they can all get a look at him? 'Lady Lucas quieted [their] fears a little by starting the idea of his being gone to London only to get a large party for the ball; a report soon followed that Mr Bingley was to bring twelve ladies and seven gentlemen with him to the assembly. The girls grieved over such a number of ladies, but were comforted the day before the ball by hearing, that instead of twelve, he had brought only six with him from London, his five sisters and a cousin. And when the party entered the assembly room, it consisted of only five altogether.' Mr Bingley has rather improved the ratio of single women to single men in that room – typical of his kind and considerate behaviour. This makes it even more rude of Mr Darcy to refuse to dance with almost all of them. Single men were a rare and valuable commodity but they were a waste of space if they refused to dance.

The scarcity of men resulted in women sometimes dancing with each other. Anything was to be preferred to sitting at the side of the room, advertising one's uninvited state. Even Mr Bennet seems aware of this when he teases his daughter Kitty by telling her, after Lydia's elopement, that 'Balls will be absolutely prohibited, unless you stand up with one of your sisters.' Jane Austen commonly saw 'a couple of ladies standing up together'.

Jane Austen is not asked to dance

Jane Austen knew that finding a partner was a matter of luck and sometimes she was forced to endure the state of being a wallflower (although that term was not one she would have known – it came into use in the Victorian era). At a ball she attended in 1800 'there was a scarcity of Men in general, & a still greater scarcity of any that were good for much', she complained. In 1808, at a Southampton ball, she reported to her sister that 'the melancholy part was to see so many dozen young Women standing by without partners'. At Hurstbourne Park she had to miss three dances for want of a partner. Believing a dance should never be wasted she often stood up with friends such as Cathcrine Bigg.

Sometimes, of course, she chose not to dance, rather than endure an unpleasant partner: 'One of my gayest actions was sitting down two Dances in preference to having Lord Bolton's eldest son for my Partner, who danced too ill to be endured.'

'Offended two or three young ladies'

Dancing and music

'Inferior to the cotillions of my own day'
Letter from Jane Austen, 1817

The boulanger

This dance went under various names – 'boulanger', 'boulangeries' and 'la boulangère' – and was a circular dance performed at the end of an evening. The name means 'The Baker's Wife' and is a joke about the baker's wife being away dancing with many other men while he was out delivering his bread. The women in the dance turned to all the other men in the set, so the dance reflected the idea nicely. Couples stood in a circle and one dancer at a time would then skip round the circle turning each male dancer alternately with her own partner. This alternated with a floor pattern where all the couples circled clockwise, then anticlockwise. The music was fast and each woman was almost hurled from one man's arms to the next (Louisa Musgrove, happy to fall into Captain Wentworth's arms, would have loved dancing the boulanger with him!) Plenty of fun was had by all, and the evening therefore ended on a high.

Jane Austen danced the boulanger at Goodnestone (the home of her sister-in-law Elizabeth, who had married Edward Austen). In a 1796 letter she reported to Cassandra: 'We dined at Goodnestone, and in the evening danced two country-dances and the Boulangeries.' Spirited women, such as Elizabeth Bennet, who runs and climbs over stiles, and Jane Austen herself, who loved a good long walk and energetic activity, were given an opportunity in this dance to really kick up their heels. Other energetic women, Jane Austen's cousins Eliza de Feuillide and Philadelphia Walters, danced the boulanger at Tunbridge Wells as the last dance of an evening ending at 2 a.m.

The Meryton assembly ball ends with this dance, and Mrs Bennet, on her return home, excitedly tells her husband just what dances Mr Bingley danced and who his partners were. 'Then, the two third he danced with Miss King, and the two fourth with Maria Lucas, and the two fifth with Jane again, and the two sixth with Lizzy, and the Boulanger—'. But Mr Bennet interrupts his wife, impatient with this recital of dance partners, so Mr Bingley's partner for the boulanger remains a permanent secret within *Pride and Prejudice*.

Country dances

When Elizabeth I went on tour through her realm, she watched with pleasure her subjects dancing on their village greens. She herself was very partial to dancing, so introduced these dances to her court. These were the origins of country dancing in England (though the name comes not from 'country' as in rural, but from the French *contredanse*, referring to the way the dancers faced each other). By the time of Charles II, another enthusiastic royal dancer, country dances were well established. John Playford, in 1651, published *The English Dancing Master*, a collection of old and new country dances, which remained in print well into the

1700s. Other publishers jumped on the bandwagon and made money from their dance manuals, and dancing masters were readily available to give lessons. Diarist Samuel Pepys, eager to learn whatever was in fashion, hired a master to teach him and his wife the latest steps. Between 1730 and 1830, 27,000 country dances and their tunes were published in England alone. By Jane Austen's lifetime, country dancing was pre-eminent. Thomas Wilson called it 'the national Dance of the English', practised 'in every city and town throughout the United Kingdom'. When we imagine Jane Austen and her characters dancing, most of the time they were executing country dances. They remained in fashion until the 1830s and 1840s – Charles Dickens described one being danced at Mr Fezziwigg's ball in *A Christmas Carol*.

Of course, the country dance changed over time. What Samuel Pepys learned was very different from the dances enjoyed by Catherine Morland and Henry Tilney. However, the essential format of dancing couples weaving their way through a variety of patterns remained the same. Each dancer had to learn precisely choreographed movements that combined with the steps of fellow dancers to create a pleasing and graceful shape to the dance as a whole. Thomas Wilson disliked movements that generated angular lines: 'Straight lines are useful, but not elegant; and, when applied to the Human Figure, are productive of an extremely ungraceful effect.' He encouraged good posture, curved arm movements, lightness of step and fans held at appropriate angles, to add to the general attractiveness of the pattern.

The country dances familiar to Jane Austen were all longways, with long lines of couples facing each other, rather than dancing in squares. Assembly rooms were long and narrow to accommodate formations and numbers of dancers. The actual steps involved were simple and few, with variety achieved by the different shapes and patterns created across the floor by the dancing couples. By the early eighteenth century, steps had become quite balletic, with rising on to points of toes, hops, leaps, and jetés all part of the performance. These were known as 'opera-steps' after the opera dances of London. Jumping, clapping, bowing and curtseys were all regular parts of country dancing.

Those dancing a country dance did not all start moving when the music began. The couple at the top (closest to the musicians) went first and danced with couples two and three. After one turn through the dance, that first couple then danced with couples three and four, leaving couple two standing out or waiting, until more turns gave them another opportunity to move again. This resulted in couples standing for some time with nothing to do but flirt, or look about, or listen (and also resulted in the phrase 'to stand up with' somebody, meaning to dance with them). Emma and her partner are waiting their turn when Emma sees Mr Elton's rudeness to Harriet: 'she was not yet dancing; she was working her way up from the bottom, and had therefore leisure to look around, and by only turning her head a little, she saw it all'. Mr Bingley first spots beautiful Jane Bennet as she is 'going down the dance' with someone else, and determines to ask her to dance with him. The dance continued until that first couple had worked its way back to the very beginning of the set.

The greater the number of dancers involved, the longer the set. Catherine Morland speaks of a dance of 'half an hour', but longer dances of up to an hour were not unknown. In a large assembly, it was especially important to secure a pleasant partner as you were stuck with that person for a very long time (imagine a whole hour with Mr Collins as your partner!). It was not unknown for dancers who had finished their own active role to go off and sit down, but this was considered selfish and ill-mannered, a breaking of the social contract. Country dances were community-minded activities – everyone danced with many different couples, and there was time to chat with many others. You were part of a group that worked together to achieve something that spectators could watch with pleasure.

With no microphone on hand to announce, in a very noisy room, which dance had been selected by the leading couple, it was important to watch carefully. The first lady would announce to those nearest her in line what the patterns of the dance were to be and what tune would be played. This meant that further along the line, couples had to observe the sequence and work out which steps to perform when it came to their turn. Thomas Wilson stressed the importance of being a leading couple: 'The persons who take upon themselves the CALLING OF THE DANCE should possess the necessary requisites for performing the duty they may have to execute, in setting the company an example, and directing them (when required) in the performance of the Dance. Such a Dance should be called, as they thoroughly understand, and are able to perform with facility. When part of the company are indifferent Dancers, the persons forming the Dance should be selected and placed according to their talent and knowledge of Dancing.' If the couple who called the dance then found they were unable to perform it, they were permitted to call another. But if the same difficulty occurred, they then had to go off to the bottom of the set and let some other couple make the calls.

Callers often called two dances in the same formation and these were danced immediately after each other. Hence Mr Bingley dances the 'two third' with Miss King, and the next 'two fourth' with Maria Lucas, while Edmund asks Fanny to save 'two dances' for him. All the country dances were in what is today called 'triple minor' format (i.e. subsets of three couples). Jane Austen never describes any country dance in detail; she assumed familiarity in all her readers and so had no need to. Nor does she ever mention a country dance by name. Surely, with her love of the navy, she'd have happily danced 'Nelson's Victory', but we have no way of knowing if she ever measured the steps for the charmingly named 'Butter'd Peas', 'Shaking of the Sheets' or 'Tippety Witchett'.

The cotillion

The cotillion (or 'cotillon', referring to the French word for petticoat and its flash as the dancers turned) arrived in England in 1766 from France, where it began as an eighteenth-century contredanse. Robert Burns mentions it in his great 1790 poem 'Tam o' Shanter' as being 'brent [brand] new frae France', but by Jane Austen's twenties it was becoming rather old-fashioned and was being replaced by the quadrille. Her niece Fanny Knight once sent her sheet music for quadrille tunes, and Aunt Jane wrote to thank her: 'Much obliged for the quadrilles, which I am grown to think pretty enough, though of course they are inferior to the Cotillions of my own day.' She clearly had fond memories of dancing cotillions – perhaps with Tom Lefroy?

Catherine Morland dances at a cotillion ball in Bath (which offered the dance long after other assembly rooms had ceased to do so), and there the cotillion opens the evening. It was a lively dance so was placed early in the programme when energy levels were high. Catherine would have joined a square of four couples, and they would all have danced a figure and a series of changes. These changes included an 'allemand', where partners cross hands behind each other's backs. This move resulted in closer physical contact than was usual in most country dances, and also gave opportunities to exchange glances over the shoulder of one's partner. As *The Mirror of the Graces* reported, 'the rapid changes of the cotillion are admirably calculated for the display of elegant gayety'. In other words, this dance was not altogether unprovocative! Sometimes cotillions included various games, with an extra man or woman being placed in the middle of the square formation. That person's job was to snatch away someone else's partner during the figures of the dance. This added to the general hilarity of the evening, though Catherine Morland would not have been pleased to have had Henry Tilney taken away from her. It sounds more like an ideal role for Isabella Thorpe.

Thomas Wilson, dancing master, provided instruction for the cotillion in his dance manuals. Catherine would have learned there how she and her partner must take their place along one side of the dance square (although the set often grew more circular in shape once the couples had taken their places), and then they'd remember for the rest of the dance their position as top couple, bottom couple, second couple (on the right) or fourth couple (on the left). Keeping her correct place in the set as she danced through the figures – and the nine or ten changes (simpler patterns among the more elaborate footwork) that went with

them – was vital, and Wilson stressed the importance of 'always preserving the Figure of the Dance'. The dance was usually four different floor patterns with a 'chorus' in between each. The chorus did not vary and was often very simple, such as circling round and back to be ready for the next figure. There was great opportunity for fancy steps, especially when standing in the middle. Based on ballet, these more intricate steps originated from Louis XIV's love of ballet and the lessons he took. Those who would otherwise be simply standing and waiting could use these steps for 'setting' to partners. Setting is a movement of greeting or honouring, which begins a dance or the next part of a dance. You face your partner and do a side-together-side-hop movement, first to your right and then to your left. The partner may or may not respond, depending on the dance. (There's a good example of this in the 1995 BBC *Pride and Prejudice*, when Lizzy dances with Mr Collins at the Netherfield ball.) Catherine would not have 'walked' such steps, but performed them with a spring. When General Tilney admires the elasticity of her walk, 'which corresponded exactly with the spirit of her dancing', it is probably her dancing of the cotillion that he has in mind.

The minuet

When James Edward Austen-Leigh tried to give an idea of his Aunt Jane's youthful frolics, he described the dances of that era: 'The stately minuet still reigned supreme; and every regular ball commenced with it. It was a slow and solemn movement, expressive of grace and dignity, rather than of merriment. It abounded in formal bows and courtesies, with measured paces, forwards, backwards and sideways and many complicated gyrations.' James would have been more exact had he been speaking of the dancing days of his grandparents, or of the balls enjoyed by Miss Gardiner before she became Mrs Bennet, or the Miss Wards of *Mansfield Park* before their marriages.

This formal dance originated in France (its name comes from the French *menuet*, meaning small or delicate) and was very popular at the court of Louis XIV. From there it made its way across the Channel to English ballrooms. However, the dance was effectively killed off in France when the aristocrats who danced it lost their heads to the guillotine. Those French aristocrats who fled to England kept it going there a little longer, but by Jane Austen's youth it had become unfashionable and young people thought it dull. It always involved the same steps, with the dancers just executing them to different tunes.

In 1816 Thomas Wilson was still insisting that it was the 'most fashionable and proper dance for the opening of a ball', but dance masters like Wilson had a stake in keeping the minuet alive. It was a complex dance – all those 'forwards, backwards and sideways' were not easy to acquire on one's own and, according to some, took up to three months to learn. The minuet continued to be taught even when out of vogue because it was considered useful in providing a good basis for elegance in dance movements. Dance manual author Nicholas Dukes described it as 'the Ground work of all other dancing'. To some observers, the minuet was 'the perfection of all dancing'.

In Bath and other cities where the population was elderly, the minuet lasted longer than in fashionable towns. It was usual for Bath balls to be opened with a minuet well into the nineteenth century. Catherine Morland goes to a 'dressed ball' in *Northanger Abbey*, and this would have had minuets to open and perhaps also before supper, so Catherine would have seen the dance even if she did not perform it herself. While minuets were not included in the Basingstoke assemblies of Jane Austen's youth, the Prince Regent gave a grand ball in 1813 that began and ended with a minuet. It was a dance for groups of couples, but when

the waltz gave couples an opportunity to move physically closer to each other and ignore others in the group, the formal, passionless minuet no longer stood a chance.

The quadrille

Descendant of the cotillion, the quadrille was also a dance for four couples in a square formation, but unlike the cotillion the formation was strictly maintained as a square. Each set had four or five figures, which were, in effect, separate dances, each with a distinctive kind of music and name, with a simple chorus in between. A greater ability to remember the figures was therefore required and the skills of the dancer much put to the test. Mr Collins would have been hopelessly challenged by the quadrille, for many quite accomplished dancers felt nervous about performing it. The steps were quite balletic and a person needed to be light of foot. 'The dancer must glide through the figures in a waving, flowing, and graceful manner', wrote one advisor. Practice was needed if the various chassés and jetés were to be performed without awkwardness.

The quadrille came seriously into fashion in the late 1810s and it dominated in many ballrooms during the nineteenth century. Captain Gronow in his *Reminiscences* noted its first appearance at Almack's: 'It was not until 1815 that Lady Jersey introduced from Paris the favourite quadrille, which has so long remained popular. I recollect the persons who formed the very first quadrille that was ever danced at Almack's.' It was slightly military in style, with marching and forming orderly lines, and this suited the times, with England at war with France. Nor did it have the more ballet-like steps of the cotillion, which made it easier, and

MARQUIS OF WORCESTER.   LADY JERSEY.   CLANRONALD MACDONALD.   LADY WORCESTER.

THE FIRST QUADRILLE AT ALMACK'S.

probably accounted for it replacing the cotillion in English ballrooms.

The provinces were always behind London fashions, so while Jane Austen possibly saw the quadrille danced in country balls she attended in the last years of her life, she herself never danced it. She played quadrille tunes on her pianoforte, but none of her characters are ever made to dance them within the pages of her novels.

The reel

Forty years after the Scottish Jacobite Rebellion (a failed attempt to overthrow George III in 1745), the English finally began to forgive the Scots and things Gaelic became romantic and fashionable. Sir Walter Scott's *Minstrelsy of the Scottish Border* and Burns's songs started a strong public interest throughout Britain in Scottish tunes and dances such as reels and strathspeys, a strathspey being a slower, more stately version of the hornpipe. The names of these new dances were delightfully Celtic – such as 'New Tartan Pladdie', 'Paddy O'Rafferty' and 'Ranting Highlanders'.

Miss Bingley, at Netherfield, plays a 'lively Scotch air' and Mary Bennet plays Scottish dance tunes at the Lucases. These were either Scottish country dances or threesome and foursome reels. The reel was a noisy dance, as it involved men, and sometimes ladies, too, raising one or both arms above their heads (a movement that imitated the antlers of a stag in rutting season), snapping their fingers, and uttering a yell or 'heuch' (a remnant of the guttural Scots' battle cry, designed to put terror into the English foe). The reel, in its basic form, consisted of three or four people in a line, alternating between performing a 'hey' (an inter weaving figure) and fancy stepping. Thomas Wilson wrote for his London pupils some very complicated reels for up to six people, but the ones danced at the Lucases would have been simpler versions. Even with simple reels, Camilla in *Catharine, or The Bower* thinks it necessary to practise her 'Scotch steps about the room' before she goes to a ball.

At Netherfield, as Miss Bingley tries to capture the attention of Mr Darcy by her fashionable playing of Italian airs and then of Scottish tunes, Darcy turns away from her to Elizabeth: "'Do not you feel a great inclination, Miss Bennet, to seize such an opportunity of dancing a reel?" She smiled, but made no answer.' Perhaps Elizabeth is imagining the reserved Mr Darcy enthusiastically performing 'Ranting Highlanders' and 'heuching' with his arms in the air. He is forced to repeat the question. "'Oh!' said she, "I heard you before, but I could not immediately determine what to say in reply. You wanted me, I know, to say 'Yes', that you might have the pleasure of despising my taste; but I always delight in overthrowing those kind of schemes. . . . I have therefore made up my mind to tell you, that I do not want to dance a reel at all – and now despise me if you dare.'"

This is an odd exchange. Reels needed more than two people involved to take place at all, so Darcy could hardly have danced it only with Elizabeth. Clearly, he is strongly attracted to her and wanting somehow to get physically closer to her, something which dancing would bring about. Italian airs provided no dancing opportunity, but Scottish tunes give him an opening, which Darcy is not slow to use. Elizabeth hesitates in responding, but he will not let the chance slip by and so repeats his question. Elizabeth is puzzled as to what to say to him. She wants to make the most of any chance to needle him, to show him her disapproval. Yet, at the same time it is strangely important to her that he does not express disapprobation of her person or her conduct – her attraction to him at this time is still a subconscious one, but this little exchange hints at it. She accuses him of wanting to despise her. Yet, while reels were popular dances, they were not common or vulgar ones. They were danced at Almack's with orchestras especially brought down from Edinburgh, and were regularly danced by the highest echelons of society. In assuming that Darcy will think less of her if she does wish to dance a reel, perhaps Elizabeth thinks that he suspects her of being like her younger sisters, who are desperate to dance on every occasion, eager to lift their arms and 'heuch' at any time, and that he will despise her for this assumed resemblance to Kitty and Lydia. Or does she think he simply abhors dancing in general (after all, 'every savage can dance', although Elizabeth never heard him make that comment)? That she is uncertain of his intention and of her own response is indicated by her long silence before replying. Elizabeth and Darcy never do get to dance a reel together.

The waltz

It was the Duke of Wellington's dashing officers who brought the waltz from Europe into England. On continental campaigns they enjoyed holding pretty girls and whirling them about the room. Napoleon

learned how to waltz to impress his wife-to-be Marie Louise of Austria. The arrival of the waltz in England in 1815 caused considerable commotion, with many regarding it as a scandalous form of public embrace. Lord Byron wrote of 'Hands which may freely range in public sight', and the *Lady's Magazine* cautioned young women against the dance. Newspapers even reported that the excitement of waltzing was so great that it caused women to faint, and as late as 1825 it was still being considered by some to be a riotous and even indecent dance. But Thomas Wilson, who published *A Description of the Correct Method of Waltzing* in 1816, insisted that the dance was 'not an enemy of true morals' and would not 'endanger virtue'. It was not then as intimate a dance as it is today – couples did not hold on to each other as we do now.

Jane Austen was never able to test her own virtue by waltzing. She missed her chance at this lovely dance, which has remained popular ever since. And when she describes Mrs Weston sitting down to play 'an irresistible waltz' that does not mean that Frank Churchill and Emma were dancing in each other's arms (which really would have disturbed Jane Fairfax!) It was simply a country dance tune in three/four time that Mrs Weston played. As the waltz was a dance especially associated with Romanticism and the sensibility movement, it is a great pity that Marianne and Willoughby are not permitted by their creator to dance it at Barton Park. Its risqué character would have suited them nicely.

The waltz brought a fundamental change to English dancing. Until this time dance had been a team effort, with partners working within a set formation with other couples. In a waltz, a man and woman turned inwards to each other, away from other couples, and had no obligation to keep to a pattern with other dancers, but could just rotate endlessly in a path of their own. Nor could they converse with others on the dance floor. The waltz made dancing more individual, part of the cultivation of personal and romantic sensibility. No longer was it such a community activity. The waltz satisfied new needs within society.

Learning new dances

When a dancing master came to a neighbourhood such as Meryton, he taught all the young people in the area the same dances. Those dances would be included at all local events for the next months, until someone who had travelled brought back the latest steps for all to enjoy, or another dancing master introduced his new dances to extend the local repertoire. Thomas Wilson would have created his own dances for his pupils, although some dances could also have been made in his name as a way of honouring him. 'Mr Beveridge's Maggot', a dance popular in Jane Austen film versions though not one danced in her lifetime, was either thought up by dance instructor Mr Beveridge or constructed in his honour by a former pupil.

Jane Austen refers to remarkably few dances by name in her fiction and in her letters. Many could have been so familiar a part of country ballrooms that she hardly needed to name them, especially to her sister who would have known just what was danced at Steventon or Basingstoke. Or dances were perhaps made up on the spot from figures everyone present knew. If they all knew the basic floor patterns – lead up and back, siding, arming, hands-around (circle), hands-across (star), hey, cast off, and whether the dance was set and cross, set and cast, or set and turn, then they could all join in and have fun. The 'first lady' was always there to remind those who forgot, and perhaps a brief reminder was sometimes written on a lady's fan. Fancy steps were not compulsory – one could manage without them. Generally they were executed by those anxious to show off. Mr Collins is too full of his own importance to make any note or even consider that he needs to remember the proper formation and the simplest of steps, which reveals a lot about his character. Knowing the dance type and performing it accurately and elegantly were vital parts of one's social duty in Jane Austen's lifetime. She herself once wrote that 'an artist cannot do anything slovenly', so we can be sure that her own dancing was everything it should be.

Dancing a reel

'Do you not feel a great inclination, Miss Bennet, to seize such an opportunity of dancing a reel?' Mr Darcy asks Elizabeth when they are at Netherfield. Elizabeth replies that she has no such inclination. The dance Darcy suggests was one that involved either two ladies and one gentleman, or two gentlemen and one lady. When Darcy poses the question, Miss Bingley and her sister are at the piano, and Mr Bingley and Mr Hurst are playing cards. Had they got up to dance the reel, Miss Bingley might have played the music; she has already started a 'lively Scotch air', which is what puts the idea of a reel into Darcy's head. Would Mrs Hurst be the extra lady in the dance, or would Mr Bingley need to be disturbed at his game of piquet to make the extra gentleman? Perhaps all these complications persuade Elizabeth to insist that she does not wish to dance.

The characters would have known the steps, for the reel was a popular dance. Thomas Wilson in his *An Analysis of Country Dancing* provides instructions so anyone could learn 'without the aid of a Master'. These diagrams show how that reel would have been danced had Elizabeth given Mr Darcy a different answer.

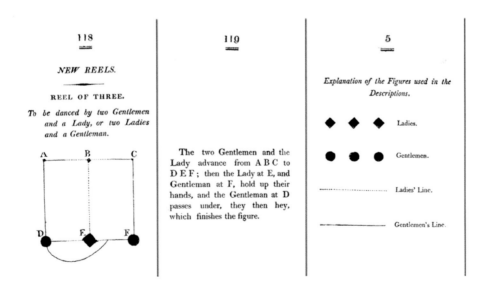

118

NEW REELS.

REEL OF THREE.

To be danced by two Gentlemen and a Lady, or two Ladies and a Gentleman.

119

The two Gentlemen and the Lady advance from A B C to D E F; then the Lady at E, and Gentleman at F, hold up their hands, and the Gentleman at D passes under, they then hey, which finishes the figure.

5

Explanation of the Figures used in the Descriptions.

Ladies.

Gentlemen.

Ladies' Line.

Gentlemen's Line.

Music to dance to

Mr Bingley thinks first of white soup when he plans to give a ball, but he ought really to have been thinking of something more important to the success of the evening – the musicians. Thomas Wilson wrote of musicians: 'that they are a useful class of persons will not be doubted; for whatever opinion has been, or may be hereafter formed of them, there is one thing certain, that there is no Dancing without them, as the Music must always guide the Dancer'.

Different sorts of balls or dances required different standards and status of musicians. Grand balls, such as those Jane Austen attended at Hurstbourne Park, and public assembly balls, employed professional

musicians. About five or six men made up the usual orchestra, and their instruments included a violin or two, pianoforte, possibly a cello or bassoon, flute or clarinet, and sometimes even a strange-looking instrument called a tenor serpent (which became popular in the early 1800s). A small one of these can be seen in the musicians' quarter of the Netherfield ball in the 1995 BBC film of *Pride and Prejudice*. The diary of John Knyveton mentions a ball he attended in London in 1794 where the orchestra consisted of 'four violins, a taber [drum], two pipes and a French horn'. Christopher Anstey in *The New Bath Guide* mentions a hautboy (a woodwind instrument which was a forerunner of the oboe), bass and fiddle at a Bath ball.

Groups of musicians travelled the countryside seeking work at local events. It was a hard life, and Thomas Wilson wrote of them with sympathy: 'Musicians are seldom paid for their playing, without their Employers complaining of the high price of their labour; yet these Employers never think that the Musicians cannot find employment for more than five or six months in the Year, and that generally in the winter Season, when the weather is bad, and their employment being principally

THE MUSICIANS' GALLERY

at night, from leaving warm rooms and being exposed afterwards to the bad effects of night air, and consequently severe colds, together with the want of rest, in a few years their constitutions are destroyed or ruined, and they are rendered totally unfit for business.' It is such men who would have been employed at the Meryton assembly, the Netherfield ball, by the Westons at the Crown Inn, by Sir Thomas Bertram at Mansfield Park, and at the Upper and Lower Rooms in Bath. Emma Watson, entering the room for the ball in the town of D., is alarmed at first to hear only the 'first scrape of one violin', but fortunately she is soon assured of there being good music for the night upon 'the orchestra's striking up a favourite air'. Sometimes it was difficult to spot the musicians when entering the ballroom – they were often discreetly hidden behind ornamental shrubbery so that fine guests did not have to gaze upon such lowborn menials as musicians!

These musicians were not always treated well. Thomas Wilson criticizes those who employed musicians and then treated them contemptuously or 'worse than their servants', and those who became overly familiar with them and 'ply them with Liquor' to make them drunk. In some ballrooms they were separated from the attendees in a minstrels' gallery, but more often in Jane Austen's time they played in a corner of the room or on a raised dais. Given their hard life – uncertain employment, no pension when they retired, low pay and low status – it is to be hoped that at the end of the Netherfield ball Mr Bingley had his carriage take the musicians to their homes so that the men and their instruments were not exposed to a cold walk after providing dance music into the early hours of the morning.

Jane Austen's novels, however, also depict more informal dances and at those no professionals were employed. Instead, a lady present would oblige the company by providing dance music for the others. Music

was an important part of a young lady's education, and playing for others part of her social obligation, but it is interesting that the women in Jane Austen's novels who play dance music either are married or consider themselves (or are so considered by others) to be unmarriageable. At the Coles' dinner party Mrs Weston seats herself at the piano to play country dance tunes, so that Emma, Frank, Jane and Harriet can all dance to them. Her courting days are over. Anne Elliot in *Persuasion* thinks hers are over, too, and so prefers 'the office of musician to a more active post' and plays country dance tunes by the hour so that the Misses Musgrove and Misses Hayter can dance. She is signalling, by so doing, that she is no longer in the marriage market. Little wonder that Captain Wentworth asks so anxiously if Miss Elliot ever dances. And in *Pride and Prejudice* Mary Bennet, highly unlikely to get a partner herself, avoids the embarrassment of being a wallflower by playing 'Scotch and Irish airs' so that her sisters can dance with the officers. Miss Bingley is at one time seen practising a 'lively Scotch air' – perhaps she too is in training for this mark of spinsterhood? Jane Austen almost certainly played music for young nieces and nephews to hop around to, but her letters make no mention of her ever playing for others at a formal dance.

Servants with musical abilities were highly valued, as they could be called on to provide music whenever the whim for dancing took hold. In *Mansfield Park* the impromptu dance that takes place in Sir Thomas's absence is possible because of 'the late acquisition of a violin player in the servants' hall'. The Bertram sisters know how to play, but neither wants to miss out on the chance to dance with Henry Crawford, and Fanny's musical education has been neglected – she cannot play the piano – so such a servant is a most welcome asset. Tradesmen living nearby who were musical and eager to earn a few extra pennies were also frequently called on. The novelist Thomas Hardy had a musical father, who taught his young son the fiddle, and together they were often called upon to play at informal dances in the neighbourhood – Hardy reflects on the experience in his *Under the Greenwood Tree*. One young lady of the period recalled in her journal how 'often, when we dined at Court, [Lady Winnington] would send for the miller, who played the violin, and set us all to dance'. The Middletons of *Sense and Sensibility* may well have similar talent below stairs or near Barton Park. When Lady Middleton, on the spur of the moment, gives 'a small dance of eight or nine couple' at Barton Park, there are 'two violins' available at a moment's notice.

What calibre of musicians were found to provide that important music for a dance depended on the formality of the occasion, the wealth of the host and the talent that was available locally, either from the company assembled or from the servants of the house. Obviously this resulted in very mixed abilities. Some were professional, properly trained and able to keep time. They played the latest tunes such as 'The Handsome Couple' and 'Revenge', performing them without mistakes. The amateurs were a more mixed bunch. When the urge to dance struck and the carpets were rolled aside, dancing to music played by Mrs Weston or Anne Elliot must have been a pleasure. But a pianist stumbling through her piece, stopping and starting, must have soon put an end to any desire for a country dance, even for those most indefatigable dancers Kitty and Lydia Bennet.

Ball Supper for Twenty People.

Roast Fowls

Millefeuille		Basket
Fricandeau	Dress Plate	Galanteens
Marangles	Raised Pie	Marangles
Ham	Dress Plate	Ham
Jelly	Roast Lamb	Blancmange
Lobster	Savoy Cake	Prawns
Cheesecakes		Custards
Roast Fowls	Frame	Roast Fowls
Custards		Tartlets
Prawns		Lobster
Blancmange	Savoy Cake	Jelly
Ham	Roast Fowls	Ham
Marangles	Dress Plate	Marangles
Galanteens	Raised Pie	Fricandeau
Basket	Dress Plate	Millefeuille
	Roast Lamb	

D E S E R T.

Lemon Ice

Pine	Frame	Peaches
Rasberry Ice		Rasberry Ice
Peaches		Grapes

Orange Ice

'They sat down to supper'

'A private dance, without sitting down to supper, was pronounced an infamous fraud upon the rights of men and women…'

EMMA

When Mr Bingley decides to host a ball at Netherfield, the first thing he thinks of is what to serve. Ball suppers reflected on the splendour of an event. Mr Bingley is new in the neighbourhood, so needs to impress his guests by offering expensive and plentiful food at his ball.

Balls generally began at 8 or 9 p.m. and the dancers would only sit down to table after three or four hours of energetic dancing. By then they must have been greatly in need of sustenance. In 1800 Jane Austen attended a ball that began at 10 p.m. and only offered supper at one in the morning.

Mr Bingley would also have given thought to the importance of the supper dance. When the dance before supper ended, a gentleman accompanied his partner into the supper room, sat talking with her while they ate, and plied her with the best things from the table. The supper dance was therefore one of the most important dances of the evening and a wonderful courtship opportunity. Mr Bingley would aim to spend extra time with Jane Bennet by asking her for the supper dance. At the Crown Inn ball in *Emma*, Frank Churchill manoeuvres so that he leaves the supper room with Jane Fairfax on one arm and Miss Bates on the other, then sits with them while they eat. Mr Knightley does not manage so well and is far removed from Emma when they sit down to supper.

Suppers had not always been an important part of a ball, food having been seen as incidental to the purpose of the evening. When the Crown Inn was built 'suppers had not been in question' and so it has no room for the purpose. But when fashionable Vauxhall Gardens added a supper room in 1786, the idea caught on and by 1814 such a facility was considered essential in any stylish assembly room, such as the one at Meryton. Only the provincial and rather dowdy Crown is still without one. However, arrangements are made by the Westons to convert a room for the purpose, for Mrs Weston's suggestion of doing without supper and only having sandwiches is pronounced 'an infamous fraud upon the rights of men and women'.

Suppers were useful courting opportunities for young people, but they must also have been eagerly anticipated by the older people in the room. Hot drinks, wine and substantial food helped fortify anxious mothers such as Mrs Bennet and Lady Lucas, card-playing gentlemen such as Mr Bennet and the various chaperones yawning on their couches.

So what was on the menu at these suppers? Soup, of course, as Mr Bingley promises. But he also provides 'cold ham and chicken' for his guests. Poached salmon was often served, along with vegetables, salads, fruit, biscuits, cheeses and cakes. Jellies served at the Mansfield ball were so plentiful that Mrs Norris is able to take the 'supernumerary' ones home with her. Usually two separate courses were considered de rigueur. *The Housekeeper's Instructor*, a best-selling cookbook of 1807, suggests a two-course ball supper menu for twenty people. This includes lobster, prawns, roast fowl, roast lamb, a variety of pies, sweet pastries, tartlets and custards, then dessert choices of pineapples (a high-status-symbol fruit of the time), grapes, peaches, and raspberries, finished off with a selection of ices. All these delicacies would be spread over the table in a pleasing arrangement, but one could only help oneself to the dishes within reach. Hence the importance to a lady of a helpful gentleman partner who could reach tasty dishes too far away to get for herself.

To drink there was lemonade for young ladies, tea, coffee, wine (sweet Madeira was especially popular), ratafia (a liqueur or cordial flavoured with fruit or nuts) or orgeat (orange syrup with almond flavouring). The Georgian era was one of very heavy drinking, and it was not uncommon for people to over-imbibe at balls. Jane Austen was delighted at an 1801 ball to observe a Mrs Badcock 'run round the room after her drunken Husband. – His avoidance, & her pursuit, with the probable intoxication of both, was an amusing scene.'

The Bennets would have been better fed at the Netherfield ball than at a Meryton assembly. Public balls were far less generous with their suppers. Tea only is served at the Upper Rooms in Bath when Catherine Morland goes to dance there, and she is so 'excessively hungry' that she has to go home and eat something before bed. At a ball in Southampton Jane Austen had to pay 'an additional shilling' for tea. Almack's in London was famously stingy with food – no alcohol was served, and the stale sandwiches and dry cakes made the place legendary for bad suppers.

Negus

Negus was a late-night drink, often served to ball guests before they departed into the cold of a winter's night. Invented by Colonel Francis Negus, a British courtier and fox hunter, the drink was made from wine (usually port) mixed with hot water, with lemon, calves-foot jelly and spices added for flavour; sugar was added for sweetness. It was mixed twenty minutes or so before serving so that the jelly melted and the flavours blended. In *The Watsons* Tom Musgrave happily assists 'the landlady in her bar to make fresh negus'. James Boswell was very partial to negus and mentions it often in his London diary.

Mr Bingley's Netherfield ball is held in winter, so negus is sure to have been served, which must have increased the exhilaration of the evening (perhaps it was over-imbibing of this alcoholic drink that leads Mrs Bennet, sitting down to supper, to talk so loudly and freely about her expectation 'that Jane would be soon married to Mr Bingley', much to the embarrassment of Elizabeth). Sir Thomas Bertram provides negus at his winter ball at Mansfield, and Fanny goes to her bed at the end of the evening 'feverish with hopes and fears, soup and negus'.

Jane Austen at a supper ball

Jane Austen had a good appetite and enjoyed her food. Entertaining at home in Southampton in 1808 she greatly relished the 'Widgeon, & the preserved Ginger'. Like all those who had energetically danced the night away, she was more than ready for her supper at the end of a ball.

She noted what was served – 'the supper was the same as last year's'; she took an interest in the food offered to her friends attending balls – 'Syllabub, Tea, Coffee, . . . a Hot Supper'.

Jane Austen once got slightly tipsy at a ball: 'I believe I drank too much wine last night', she told Cassandra, after attending a dance at Hurstbourne Park in November 1800. She thought this 'venial Error' on her part might account for a shaking hand as she wrote her letter. Too much of such drinking and Jane Austen might not have been able to write her novels!

White Soup

'But as for the ball', Mr Bingley tells his sisters, 'it is quite a settled thing; and as soon as Nicholls has made white soup enough I shall send round my cards.' The supper at Netherfield was probably served around midnight and after enduring two dances with Mr Collins, Elizabeth would have been more than ready for the promised soup.

White soup was made from expensive ingredients – cream, almonds and egg yolks. It was something of a status symbol – only the wealthy could offer white soup to their guests. The dish probably originated in seventeenth-century France, where it was known as Soupe à la Reine (Queen's Soup). The first known recipe there dates from 1651, and was translated into English a few years later. Frederick Nutt gives a recipe for it in *The Imperial and Royal Cook* of 1809, while *A New System of Domestic Cookery* by Mrs Rundell in 1816 gives two variants. Obviously over the years many alternatives crept into the recipe, but it was generally made by stewing together veal, chicken, bacon and herbs, and thickened with rice or breadcrumbs; then cream, almonds and eggs were added. Alcohol was occasionally an ingredient.

Soup was regarded as essential at a ball. It is served at the Mansfield Park ball which Sir Thomas puts on for Fanny Price, and Miss Bates is delighted to see it served as part of the 'elegance and profusion' of the supper at the Crown Inn. Although Miss Bates comments that 'it smells most excellent' and she 'cannot help beginning' it as soon as she sits down, she fails to tell us what sort of soup it is. It can't have been very hot by the time it was delivered from the kitchen, but guests would have been used to most food being served tepid rather than piping hot as we enjoy it today.

'Receipt for White Soup'

Put a knuckle of veal into six quarts of water, with a large fowl, and a pound of lean bacon, half a pound of rice, two anchovies, a few pepper-corns, a bundle of sweet herbs [thyme, marjoram or tarragon, tied together into a bundle], two or three onions, and three or four heads of celery cut in slices. Stew them all together, till the soup is as strong as you would have it, and then strain it through a hair sieve into a clean earthen pot: let it stand all night, skim off the fat, and pour it into a stewpan. Put in half a pound of Jordan almonds beat fine, simmer it a little, and run it through a tamis [a fine cloth sieve]: add a pint of cream and the yolk of an egg, and send it up hot.

(From John Farley's *London Art of Cooking*, 1783)

Conversation and courtship

'Do you talk by rule, then, while you are dancing?'
PRIDE AND PREJUDICE

When Mr Darcy dances with Elizabeth at the Netherfield Ball, they dance very silently for some time, until 'she began to imagine that their silence was to last through two dances'. Dancing master Thomas Wilson would have approved of this quiet behaviour. In his view, couples should either converse about the dance itself or preserve an attentive silence. 'It too frequently occurs', he complained, 'that one half of the persons composing the dance are in conversation on subjects unconnected with the dance'. It is unlikely, however, that Mr Darcy is thinking of the strictures of a dancing master as he stands silently opposite Elizabeth Bennet. His silence arises from the conflicting emotions he is experiencing. He wants to disapprove of Elizabeth and all her relations, but 'in Darcy's breast there was a tolerably powerful feeling towards her', and there is no doubt that he is strongly attracted. His mind is simply too full of all this confusion for him to supply light conversation. Elizabeth Bennet enjoys breaking the rules – walking alone, jumping over puddles and stiles, speaking her mind freely and openly. In this ball scene, she is bent on breaking Thomas Wilson's rule about silence, and decides to force Darcy to speak solely to punish him for, as she believes, keeping Wickham away.

Dancing instructors might prefer an attentive silence for dancing couples, but the reality was that every lady and gentleman was expected to have a repertoire of small talk ready for use in the ballroom. Elizabeth archly uses just such light conversation in her opening gambit against Darcy when she makes 'some slight observation on the dance'. Darcy replies briefly and again lapses into his distracted silence, but Elizabeth refuses to give up:

> 'It is your turn to say something now, Mr Darcy. – I talked about the dance, and you ought to make some kind of remark on the size of the room, or the number of couples.'

Darcy smiles at her ironic mimicry of ballroom chit-chat, and assures her 'that whatever she wished him to say should be said'.

> 'Very well. – That reply will do for the present. – Perhaps by and bye I may observe that private balls are much pleasanter than public ones. – But now we may be silent.'
>
> 'Do you talk by rule, then, while you are dancing?'
>
> 'Sometimes. One must speak a little, you know. It would look odd to be entirely silent for half an hour together; and yet for the advantage of some, conversation ought to be so arranged as that they may have the trouble of saying as little as possible.'
>
> 'Are you consulting your own feelings in the present case, or do you imagine that you are gratifying mine?'
>
> 'Both,' replied Elizabeth archly; 'for I have always seen a great similarity in the turn of our minds. – We are each of an unsocial, taciturn disposition, unwilling to speak, unless we expect to say something that will amaze the whole room, and be handed down to posterity with all the eclat of a proverb.'
>
> 'This is no very striking resemblance of your own character, I am sure', said he. 'How near it may be to mine, I cannot pretend to say. – You think it a faithful portrait undoubtedly.'
>
> 'I must not decide on my own performance.'
>
> He made no answer, and they were again silent till they had gone down the dance . . .

Elizabeth has tried to needle Darcy, and it hasn't worked. At every provocation, he has replied amiably, and he even opens new subjects of conversation himself when she grows silent. That her family has been in his thoughts is evident when he asks 'if she and her sisters did not very often walk to Meryton'. Elizabeth cannot resist! This gives her an opening to mention Mr Wickham and she has the satisfaction of getting an instant reaction: 'A deeper shade of hauteur overspread his features, but he said not a word.'

Their ensuing talk is as unlike polite social chat as it could possibly be. Elizabeth openly accuses Darcy of harming Wickham and their talk turns into a form of duelling – she attacks, and he parries. He tries to introduce a safer subject – books and their tastes in reading – but Elizabeth won't have that either: 'No – I cannot talk of books in a ball-room; my head is always full of something else.' She forces him to speak about 'resentment' and 'prejudice', subjects connected with Wickham; he wants to know why she is asking. Her response is crushing to any romantic hopes he might be starting to cherish: 'But if I do not take your likeness now, I may never have another opportunity.' In other words, 'I will probably never dance with you again.' Mortified, Darcy can only respond coldly, and they complete the dance in silence, and with dissatisfaction. She is angry with him and angry with herself for taunting him. He turns his anger against Wickham, who is fast becoming a possible rival.

This is a brilliant scene in *Pride and Prejudice*. Darcy's and Elizabeth's bodies follow the required movements of the dance, creating with the other dancers a pleasing and harmonious pattern. Their hands are clasped and they bow and curtsey to each other. In contrast, there is nothing harmonious about their conversation, and the verbal sparring between them grows heated and almost dangerous. There is no meeting of minds, as there is a meeting of hands. Elizabeth's fine eyes flash with annoyance, her wit also flashes, and she won't let Darcy get away with anything. He, usually reserved on the dance floor, is forced to speak to defend his own character against her attacks, while simultaneously struggling with a growing admiration for her and a developing jealousy of Wickham. In the end, he can only lapse into stricken silence. All this, as they dance their steps so correctly and well that Sir William Lucas interrupts to congratulate them on Darcy's 'very superior dancing' and the elegance of his partner. It is no mean feat for them both to dance well as they participate in this verbal duel.

What is also intriguing about this scene is that Darcy and Elizabeth appear to be almost alone on the dance floor. Sir William intrudes briefly, and there is a passing mention of Jane and Bingley dancing together nearby, but so strong is the focus of hero and heroine on each other that other dancers seem to fade away. No one else matters, and this sense of their solitariness within a crowd emphasizes the fact that there is no room in their minds at this time for anyone else. Each is totally taken up with the other. It is moments such as these that make their eventual love for each other so convincing.

Dancing was valued in Jane Austen's time for the chance it gave young men and women to talk without any chaperone within hearing distance. Many of her characters take advantage of this opportunity. Henry Tilney of *Northanger Abbey*, a man who loves clever conversation, entrances Catherine with his witty talk whenever he stands up with her. Henry is considerate of his partner, choosing topics that will interest her and gently teasing her at the same time. He follows the advice of conduct-book writer Dr Gregory, who advised that 'the art of pleasing in conversation consists in making the company pleased with themselves!' John Thorpe appears unacquainted with Dr Gregory's advice – he is totally lacking in conversational manners. As he dances with Catherine, he talks only of what interests *him*: 'of the horses and dogs of the friend whom he had just left, and of a proposed exchange of terriers'. Catherine, not surprisingly, is bored, and spends the dance looking about for Mr Tilney and his sister.

Conversation during dancing could be frustratingly superficial. Had Mr Bennet spoken of books to Miss Gardiner, instead of making remarks about the number of couples or that day's weather, he might have discovered before proposing to her that she 'was a woman of mean understanding, little information, and uncertain temper'. Or if Mr Palmer had tried to discuss politics with Miss Charlotte Jennings, he might never have made her Mrs Palmer. 'Deep' topics were discouraged in the ballroom, but misrepresentation or ignorance of one's partner's true character was often the consequence. There was not enough 'making out' of characters on the Regency dance floors. Yet clever people could gain a great deal of knowledge about a partner even when discussing superficial subjects. For example, Emma Watson soon learns of Mr Howard that 'though chatting on the commonest topics, he had a sensible, unaffected way of expressing himself, which made them all worth hearing'.

But not everyone could be clear-sighted in a ballroom, and Jane Austen's novels show that mistakes did occur. Too much superficial chat, or perhaps no chat at all, resulted in marriages such as the Bennets', Middletons', Palmers', Sir Walter and Lady Elliot's, Charles and Mary Musgrove's, and the various other mismatches of the novels. And sometimes conversational pointers were simply ignored. Charlotte Lucas dances and talks with Mr Collins and soon sees that he is a fool, yet she marries him all the same. Mr Rushworth must have revealed his stupidity in his first dance with Maria Bertram but she, blinded by his money, accepts his proposal soon afterwards. For most couples, ballroom conversation was all they had to go on when judging the intelligence of a possible future spouse. They simply could not pass up such valuable opportunities, which they would have done had they obeyed Thomas Wilson's rule of silence in a ballroom.

The Bennet sisters enter the Meryton assembly room with high hopes of conquering Mr Bingley's heart and know that if he loves to dance, then their chances of doing so are increased. Modern singles in search of love can try a dating service or the Internet, but Regency girls seeking eligible men headed for the nearest ballroom. In many ways a public assembly ball was the equivalent of today's speed dating. It is impossible to underestimate the importance of balls to young women such as the Bennets and Lucases. With a shortage of men and intense competition in the marriage market, every ball had to be approached strategically. Ballrooms were the fields of marital campaigns fought by mothers and their daughters. Young ladies had to be properly 'armed' and prepared. So the Bennet girls choose their best gowns, becomingly arrange their hair, and, properly chaperoned by their mother, set off to dance their way into love or marriage – hopefully both!

Mr Bingley and Jane Bennet fall in love on that first evening. Dancing works its magic on them both. He admires her beauty – 'Oh! she is the most beautiful creature I ever beheld!' – and she thinks him handsome; they talk and smile as they dance. Music can be very seductive and perhaps they danced to tunes such as 'Haste to the Wedding' or 'The Happy Marriage', bringing the idea of courtship even more to mind. Lord Byron, an expert at falling in (and out of) love, recognized the seductiveness of dance although he was only a bystander, never a participant (because of his deformed foot). In a poem describing an 1815 ball, he wrote:

> A thousand hearts beat happily; and when
> Music arose with its voluptuous swell,
> Soft eyes looked love to eyes which spake again,
> And all went merry as a marriage bell.

Jane Bennet and Mr Bingley fall in love very respectably – they do nothing improper on the dance floor. But moralists feared the romantic aspects of dancing. Conduct-book writer Thomas Gisborne declared in his *Enquiry into the Duties of the Female Sex* in 1797 that while dancing should be a healthy and innocent pastime, women could easily grow 'too elated', without 'suitable regulations' to restrain them. Dancing master Thomas Wilson insisted that physical passions had to be subdued and 'mutual purity of conduct' aimed for instead. All too easily could 'art and motion wake the sleeping fire', as another dance instructor, Mr Jenkins, warned. In other words, young people such as Jane and Bingley should not be enjoying sexual attraction in a ballroom. The moralists might grumble, but the reality for many was that 'soft eyes looked love', cheeks blushed, and lips smiled invitingly – human nature being what it is, physical attraction could not be banished from a dance. However, Jane Bennet almost loses Mr Bingley because she does not display openly enough her romantic interest in him. As Charlotte Lucas complains, Jane 'does not help him on'. Women had to manage a fine balance in such matters.

In *Northanger Abbey* the romance begins on Catherine's side. When she meets Henry Tilney she thinks he 'if not quite handsome, was very near it'. Soon she comes to feel that she is in 'high luck' to have met him and that Henry is everything a young man ought to be. When they part, she has 'a strong inclination' to see him again and, after a few more meetings, Catherine is deeply in love. Henry's attachment to her is slower to form: 'his affection originated in nothing better than gratitude, or, in other words, that a persuasion of her partiality for him had been the only cause of giving her a serious thought'.

Once he does start to think seriously of her as a possible wife, Henry reveals his awakening interest by bravely introducing the topic of matrimony into their dance conversation. He wants to probe beyond the superficial obligations of being dance partners to explore the idea of being marriage partners as well and, as David Selwyn has described it, Henry Tilney 'cleverly combines the activity they are currently performing with a projection of the more lasting partnership the novel destines for them':

> 'I consider a country-dance as an emblem of marriage. Fidelity and complaisance are the principal duties of both; and those men who do not choose to dance or marry themselves, have no business with the partners or wives of their neighbours.'
>
> 'But they are such very different things!'
>
> 'That you think they cannot be compared together.'
>
> 'To be sure not. People that marry can never part, but must go and keep house together. People that dance, only stand opposite each other in a long room for half an hour.'
>
> 'And such is your definition of matrimony and dancing. Taken in that light certainly, their resemblance is not striking; but I think I could place them in such a view. – You will allow that in both man has the advantage of choice, woman only the power of refusal; that in both, it is an engagement between man and woman, formed for the advantage of each; and that when once entered into, they belong exclusively to each other till the moment of its dissolution; that it is their duty each to endeavour to give the other no cause for wishing that he or she had bestowed themselves elsewhere, and their best interest to keep their own imaginations from wandering towards the perfections of their neighbours, or fancying that they should have been better off with any one else.'

As well as seeking out her views, Henry is creating an advertisement – for himself! He is letting her know that when he marries he intends to be a faithful husband, that he understands that 'agreement and compliance are expected from him' and will be supplied. Any marriage in which he is involved will be a contract of pleasure for each spouse. Catherine is uncertain at first, insisting on the differences while he stresses the similarities, but eventually she is able to give him the reassurance he requires when she tells him that she does 'not want to talk to any body' except him, unwittingly revealing just how much she cares. To have a pretty girl so obviously smitten with him is something Henry cannot resist. Soon he is proposing walking with her, he seeks her out at the theatre, grows offended when he mistakenly thinks she has let him down for another man, and shows every symptom of someone in love. At the novel's end Catherine was assured of Henry's affection; 'and that heart in return was solicited, which, perhaps, they pretty equally knew was already entirely his own'. Balls have created just the right romantic atmosphere for Catherine and Henry, and love and marriage are the result.

＂

In *Sense and Sensibility* there is a strong physical attraction between Marianne and Willoughby well before they dance together. Injured on the hillside, she is swept into his arms and carried home. While she blushes modestly at this close encounter, she can't wait to have Willoughby near her again and is delighted to learn that he loves to dance. When they dance together at Barton Park, they are oblivious to those around them. This is one of the most obvious courtships in any Jane Austen novel. It may be a romantic haze for Marianne, but for Willoughby it is less cerebral. A year earlier he seduced a young girl in Bath and left her pregnant; he clearly hopes to entice Marianne into his bed (this is why he takes her to Allenham, but Marianne's virtue proves too strong). Willoughby's debts make him realize he can't have money and a gorgeous wife, so he leaves Barton. Marianne is not shown formally renouncing dancing, but from that moment she is never depicted doing so again – Willoughby takes dance out of her life. In the end he opts to marry for money, while Marianne marries for prudence and affection, rather than from passion. Neither ever forgets, however, the magnetism of their dances together, or the lessons it taught them that dancing lovers do not always follow a path to matrimony.

＂

When Mr Darcy proposes to Elizabeth Bennet, he tells her: 'In vain have

I struggled. It will not do. My feelings will not be repressed. You must allow me to tell you how ardently I admire and love you.' In the dance scenes of *Pride and Prejudice* Jane Austen makes this 'struggling' and 'repression' all too clear. Mr Darcy is at war with himself. He disapproves of Elizabeth and her family; he does not want to link his aristocratic lineage with a 'nobody' from a country town. His stated dislike of dancing is indicative of his resistance to marriage. Yet Elizabeth attracts him strongly: her bright eyes, her clever repartee, the fact that she does not fawn and flatter him – all enchant him far more than he likes. He admires her graceful figure as she dances and is very aware of her physically, he notes the quick turns of her intelligent mind, she rouses him from his usual state of calm indifference, and he falls in love, in spite of himself.

Elizabeth only realizes she loves Darcy near the end of the novel, just when she thinks Lydia's elopement has driven him away from her for good. Her love has been of gradual growth, with respect and gratitude slowly eroding the prejudice she formed against him at the Meryton assembly ball. Yet at no time in the novel is Elizabeth ever indifferent to Mr Darcy and this is made very clear in all the scenes where they dance together – when he hurts her pride she has 'no very cordial feelings towards him', she resents his supposed treatment of Mr Wickham so feels an urge to provoke him. Elizabeth goes through a great variety of emotions concerning Darcy but slowly she starts to do him justice, warms to him, and finally, she loves him. Through all their courtship she remains physically very aware of his tall, imposing figure and feels a sudden new sense of importance when she stands with him on the dance floor – chemistry is there, but it takes a long time for Elizabeth to recognize it as such. When she encounters his portrait at Pemberley she stands 'several minutes before the picture', remembering that he often had just such a smile on his face looking at her. Darcy is not often described as smiling, but two of the occasions when he does so are at the Netherfield ball, and Elizabeth recalls those moments when she looks at the portrait.

Dancing is an integral part of courtship in *Pride and Prejudice*. Jane and Bingley fall quickly in love while dancing; their absorption in each other is noticed by all the bystanders, though Jane's natural reserve disguises the depth of her feelings. Bingley asks to be introduced to Jane so that he can invite her to dance. He asks her again and again, securing her hand for all remaining dances; and he stays by her side to talk when the dances end. Such 'particular' attentions from him give rise to Jane's 'happy, though modest hopes'. Bingley's sociability and pleasantness in a ballroom show Jane just what sort of man he is, and how well he would suit her own cheerful, easygoing disposition. Jane's beauty and smiles enchant Bingley, but it's the dancing that provides the magic.

𝄢

There are echoes of Henry Fielding's *Tom Jones* (the novel discussed during a dance by Jane Austen and Tom Lefroy) in *Mansfield Park*, a novel full of amorous mix-ups and incompatible couples who dance in various pairs and fall in and out of love as they do.

Henry Crawford dances and flirts with the Bertram sisters, but suddenly decides that Fanny is the girl he loves. Once he has worked that out, he is eager to dance with her and quickly engages her for the first dance of the Mansfield ball. He 'was in excellent spirits, and tried to impart them to her', but the chemistry is just not there. Fanny is in love with another, so fails to respond to Crawford's charm. All she wants to do is dance with Edmund, and she is at her happiest when those dances occur. Unfortunately for Fanny, Edmund is thinking of Mary Crawford, which makes him depressed and withdrawn – she has told him she will not dance with a clergyman and he is about to be ordained. Fanny and Edmund 'went down their two dances together with such sober tranquillity as might satisfy any looker-on, that Sir Thomas had been bringing up no wife for his younger son'.

And there are other dancers in the room who are mismatched. Maria dances with Mr Rushworth but smiles at Henry Crawford as she does so; Julia stands up with Mr Yates, who admires her, but Julia wishes he were Mr Crawford; Tom dances reluctantly with Fanny and would rather be playing billiards; and Mary won't dance with Edmund if he becomes a clergyman. The smooth flowing patterns of a dance are, metaphorically, tangled and out of step in this novel. This is also the only one of the novels to depict a married woman (Mrs Grant) dancing with single men. No courtship is advanced in the Mansfield ballroom. Instead, romances are damaged or broken apart, feet grow tired, spirits feverish and restless. The happy romantic attraction of balls in the earlier novels is woefully absent from *Mansfield Park*.

ɔɔ

Ballroom courtships are wonderfully deep, yet subtle, in *Emma*. Throughout her life Emma has never viewed Mr Knightley as a possible lover. He is a relation through marriage, an old family friend, and old enough (just) to be her father – she has never thought of him amorously. But this all changes at a ball. While dancing at the Crown Inn, she notes for the first time his upright figure and how well he compares with other men. She

starts to imagine him moving in the dance, she catches his eye and makes him smile, her thoughts flutter with awakening romantic interest. Emma has danced several times with Frank Churchill and is left quite unruffled by that experience, but the mere thought of dancing with Mr Knightley brings a whole new awareness of her own body, and of his. Is he looking at her, or not? Does he like what he sees, or does he disapprove? Harriet Smith, falling for Mr Knightley as she dances with him, has the same rush of excitement – 'she bounded higher than ever, flew farther down the middle, and was in a continual course of smiles'.

Emma feels the need to draw Mr Knightley closer – 'her eyes invited him irresistibly to come to her' – and, if possible, persuade him on to the dance floor. 'I am ready', she tells him, 'whenever I am wanted . . . You have shown that you can dance, and you know we are not really so much brother and sister as to make it at all improper.' Emma slowly begins to realize her feelings for Mr Knightley have changed. He, however, knows his own heart better and, in one of the most romantically charged moments of the novel, replies: 'Brother and sister! – no, indeed.' Old ways of viewing each other are thrown away, leaving the path clear for a new relationship.

·"

There are no dancing lovers in *Persuasion*. Jane Austen does not depict Anne and Captain Wentworth standing up with each other in any ballroom, though their original courtship must have included dances. That Anne appears to have given up dancing altogether indicates her depression and her symbolic withdrawal from the marriage market. Anne Elliot does everything neatly and well, so it is easy to imagine her as an elegant and graceful dancer. What a pity we never see her in action! The Musgrove girls are fond of dancing, and Henrietta must have often danced with her cousin Charles Hayter and so have fallen in love with him, but again such a dance is not described within the pages of the novel. Nor is Louisa ever shown dancing with Captain Benwick, another couple not falling in love on the dance floor in *Persuasion*.

The unfinished novels give only glimpses of dancing lovers. Lady Susan is never depicted dancing. Country dances involved team work, obeying the rules, waiting patiently for your turn to move, forming correct patterns along with the others in the set – and none of this suits Lady Susan, who is not at all community-minded. She would have infinitely preferred the waltz, but of course she was too early for that dance. In a waltz she could be a free spirit, enjoy closer physical contact with her partner and uninterrupted flirting with him, something that would be difficult in a country dance focused on floor patterns. The intimate waltz would have been tailor-made for Lady Susan Vernon.

According to Cassandra Austen, Mr Howard was destined to be Emma Watson's hero in *The Watsons*. They enjoy two dances together and both find them 'very short' because they are enjoying themselves so much. Clearly there is a strong mutual attraction, but little detail is provided. There is also in the same novel a rather strange, surrogate courtship of Emma by Lord Osborne, but he cannot even summon the energy or courage to dance with her himself and does his courting by proxy.

It is only the sea that dances in *Sanditon*. The unfinished manuscript never once mentions balls or even the activity of dancing – all those invalids have other physical concerns on their minds. Perhaps, had Jane Austen lived to complete it, she would have included a dance scene and depicted Charlotte Heywood with Sidney Parker. Or Mr Parker might have come to realize that providing an assembly room for young people would do far more to attract visitors to the town than would a library or fashionable doctor. Slothful Arthur Parker might have stirred himself to dance with the Miss Beauforts, and they could even have added thick, rich cocoa to the supper menu especially for him. It is sad to think that dancing, so important in all her completed novels, should be missing from this last of Jane Austen's writings.

Jane Austen falls in love at a private dance

In January 1796, at a private dance, Jane Austen fell in love. The dance was held by her friends and neighbours George and Anne Lefroy. Staying at their home was a young nephew, Thomas Lefroy, who was visiting them at their home in Ashe before beginning legal studies in London. He was a handsome young man – the miniature painted of him at about this time depicts an attractive and open face, with especially appealing eyes (and Jane Austen had a weakness for fine eyes in a man). As Jon Spence describes it in *Becoming Jane Austen*, Tom 'had large eyes and a lively expression with just a hint of shyness in it. You can see the attraction: it is a witty, mobile face. But it is immature, the face of a boy.' It must have been love at first sight, for they danced together with mutual pleasure. Luckily, it was the season for dancing: several balls were held in the neighbourhood over the Christmas period and Tom and Jane danced together at four of them. Jane's joy in this romance almost springs off the pages of the letter she wrote to Cassandra, who was away and unable to watch her little sister falling in love. 'You scold me so much in the nice long letter which I have this moment received from you, that I am almost afraid to tell you how my Irish friend and I behaved. Imagine to yourself', she gleefully instructed Cassandra, 'everything most profligate and shocking in the way of dancing and sitting down together.' She knew she was 'being particular', but she didn't care – at these balls her heart ruled her head.

Unlike Elizabeth Bennet and Mr Darcy, Jane and Tom did talk of books, and discovered a mutual enjoyment of Fielding's *Tom Jones*. Jane practised her flirting skills to the utmost and delighted in putting to shame another courting couple: 'Mr H. [William Heathcote] began with Elizabeth [Bigg], and afterwards danced with her again; but they do not know how to be particular. I flatter myself, however, that they will profit by the three successive lessons which I have given them.'

Did the flirting continue the next morning when Tom called, as custom dictated, on his dance partner of the night before? Jane certainly told Cassandra with pleasure of this morning visit. Indeed, she quite equals poor Anne Steele of *Sense and Sensibility* in her desire to be teased about this new beau and her longing to talk about him. Her small Hampshire community quickly took note of this very 'particular' dancing couple. One friend even sketched Tom for Jane, and the Lefroy family teased Tom about his new girl. Cassandra, staying at the time with her fiancé's family, heard with concern of this new man in her sister's life and wrote to caution, to dampen the excited hopes in case they came to nothing.

The day of the fourth ball arrived. It was held at Ashe and was a farewell to Tom, who was leaving for London to begin studying law. Jane was excited about this ball, knowing she would dance once more with him: 'I look forward with great impatience to it, as I rather expect to receive an offer from my friend in the course of the evening.' What happened at that vital ball? No account exists. Probably Jane danced twice with Tom, perhaps there were sighs and a sorrowful pressing of hands in the last dance they would ever perform together – we shall never know. Tom, too poor to consider marrying a penniless Hampshire girl with no connections, did not propose to Jane Austen.

Chaperones

Mrs Bennet might be a vulgar and embarrassing mother, but she knows how to do her duty as a chaperone. So does Lady Lucas, and Mrs Long who chaperones her niece. They have enjoyed their own days of dancing, and now they must ensure that their daughters are properly taken care of in the ballroom. It was their duty to remind their girls of the rules of good conduct, ensure their safety, provide advice about dress, and protect them from suitors interested solely in dowries or seduction.

Dr Johnson's dictionary, published in 1755, did not list the modern meaning of the word 'chaperon'. It originated in France where *un chaperon* was a 'hood for a hawk', and it is this meaning of the word that Dr Johnson provides in his dictionary. The French verb *chaperonner*, meaning 'to cover with a hood', also came eventually to include 'to protect' or 'to escort', and it was this meaning which made its way into English. Dr Johnson listed 'chaperon' only as a noun, and the very first recorded written use of 'to chaperon' as a verb is to be found in Jane Austen's *Sense and Sensibility*. These days an 'e' is added to the end of the word, but Jane Austen only used that once when she misspelled it as 'chaprone' in her juvenilia.

Jane Austen presents a great variety of women in this role within her fiction. First there are the mothers, doing their maternal duty by taking daughters to balls so as to find them husbands. Along with Mrs Bennet and Lady Lucas are Mrs Thorpe, Mrs Edwards and Mrs Dashwood, all sociable females who seem to gain as much enjoyment from a ball as their offspring. In fact, some of them are so busy having fun they forget their duty to protect, thus exposing their girls to the Wickhams, Captain Tilneys, Willoughbys and fortune-hunting officers of the ballroom. Nor are they all successful in finding partners for their girls. Mrs Bennet's vulgarity deters would-be suitors of Jane and Elizabeth, and Charlotte Lucas manages to make her bid for Mr Collins at the ball without her mother even noticing that she is doing so. Mrs Thorpe talks too much of her son and leaves Isabella to fend for herself, and Mrs Edwards, who chaperones Emma and Mary in *The Watsons*, seems powerless to prevent Mary from dancing the whole night with officers. They are not the most successful group of chaperones in fiction!

> 'I find many Douceurs in being a sort of Chaperon for I am put on the Sofa near the Fire & can drink as much wine as I like.'
> Letter from Jane Austen, 1813

Some mothers are reluctant to take on the role. In *A Collection of Letters*, one of Jane Austen's juvenile writings, one mother about to 'bring out' her two daughters thinks 'it would be awkward for them to enter too wide a Circle' and far too exciting for them to dance at a ball, so takes them out to drink tea instead. 'Lady Bertram did not go into public with her daughters. She was too indolent even to accept a mother's gratification in witnessing their success and enjoyment at the expense of any personal trouble, and the charge was made over to her sister, who desired nothing better than a post of such honourable representation, and very thoroughly relished the means it afforded her of mixing in society without having horses to hire.' Lady Bertram is deficient in her duty and pays a price for her negligence: the Bertram girls misbehave, to put it lightly, Julia elopes and Maria commits adultery.

Then there is a large group of married women who take charge of chaperoning other girls. Kind Mrs Allen takes Catherine Morland under her wing, Mrs Jennings and Mrs Palmer are 'very happy to chaperon' the Dashwood sisters in London, and Lady Russell escorts her goddaughter Anne Elliot. Mrs Percival, in *Catharine, or The Bower*, is an extremely strict chaperone to her niece Catharine, and Mrs Edwards is happy to do double duty by accompanying her own daughter Mary and also Emma Watson. Mrs Grant is ready and willing to escort her half sister Mary Crawford to any dance offered, and Mrs Norris looks about 'for their future husbands' when she takes her nieces to local balls. Some chaperones are very young to take on such a responsibility. Mrs Forster is only recently married when she escorts Lydia Bennet to Brighton balls and her inexperience has dreadful consequences, for Lydia elopes. The newlywed Mrs Elton tries to chaperone Jane Fairfax, feeling this will add to her own importance as a married woman, and sees herself as 'chaperon of the party' at both Box Hill and Donwell Abbey. In the juvenile piece *The Three Sisters* young Mary Stanhope hopes that one of her first duties as a married woman will be 'to chaprone Sophy and Georgiana to all the Winter Balls'.

The third group of women who perform this vital role are those paid to do so. Being either a governess or companion was not an enviable task but respectable single females often had no other option. Mrs Younge is placed in charge of Georgiana Darcy at Ramsgate, and fails abysmally in her chaperonage, while Mrs Jenkinson is a rather superfluous 'protector' of Anne de Bourgh. Jane Fairfax can envisage for herself the 'slavery' of caring for little girls who will one day need to be escorted to balls, but she is fortunately spared such a fate. Had poor Emma Woodhouse ever been given the chance to go to public balls as a young girl (her father hates the very idea of dances), she would have been accompanied there by 'poor Miss Taylor', her governess.

All these women were expected to pass the long evenings as best they could – gossiping with friends, playing cards, imbibing, eating too much supper (very portly chaperones are mentioned in *The Watsons*) or even indulging in scandalous liaisons (Jane Austen once took great delight in noticing an adulteress at a ball). They rarely danced themselves. Without the exercise of dancing to warm the limbs, sitting chaperones often suffered from the cold, so a fire at one end of the ballroom would attract a huddle of escorts. At Mansfield Park Mrs Norris tries to 'move all the chaperons at the fire' to a 'better part of the room' – a typical example of Mrs Norris's pointless meddling.

Jane Austen was very happy to be 'put on the Sofa near the Fire' when she accompanied nieces to balls. There she could drink wine, keep an eye on the proceedings, or observe courtships in progress: 'I do not know what to do about Jemima Branfill', she complained to her niece, Fanny, in 1817. 'What does her dancing away with so much spirit, mean? – that she does not care for him, or only wishes to appear not to care for him? – Who can understand a young Lady?' Yet, as a chaperone, and as a writer, she attempted to understand all the courtships that went on both before her eyes and in her vivid imagination.

Talking over Thursday night

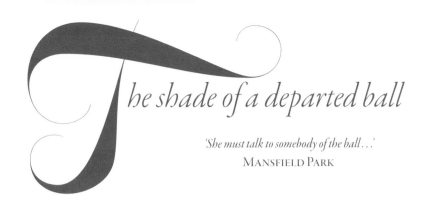

The shade of a departed ball

'She must talk to somebody of the ball…'
MANSFIELD PARK

The ball is over! The musicians have played the last dance and carriages have driven up to the front door to collect the guests and face the dark ride home. Servants, longing for their beds, have come to snuff the wax candles, collect the remains of supper and sticky cups of negus and soup, lock the doors, and make all secure. The musicians have been handed their meagre pay and have departed. The dancers leave Netherfield or the Crown Inn, the Upper Rooms of Bath or Barton Park. Balls have given them the chance to display their persons and dress, to enjoy witty conversation, to eat well, win money in the card room, or be introduced to an important connection. If very lucky, a dancer might have attracted a personable young clergyman, a handsome fellow in a scarlet coat, or even a young man worth ten thousand a year. Or have partnered a pretty girl 'wild for dancing', or one whose sparkling dark eyes were hard to forget. But the dance has ended, and with it most of the fun and enchantment of the night. But not quite . . .

'That the Miss Lucases and the Miss Bennets should meet to talk over a ball was absolutely necessary; and the morning after the assembly brought the former to Longbourn to hear and to communicate.' The Bennet sisters love such after-ball conversations. Elizabeth and Jane can enjoy wonderful post-mortems in the privacy of their bedroom (just as Jane Austen and her sister must so often have done), but they also have the Lucas girls with whom to compare notes. Mrs Bennet, who loves to gossip, joins in, and even Mary Bennet puts down her books to take part in the discussion. Mr Darcy's rudeness to Lizzy, Bingley's obvious preference for Jane, Mrs

Long's experience sitting next to Darcy at supper and Mr Darcy's wealth – all are gone over thoroughly, and with much enjoyment, by the ladies.

Many of Jane Austen's heroines share this pleasure. Even Fanny Price, not the most social or chatty of individuals, badly needs to talk over her ball and is intensely frustrated by having no sympathetic friend at hand for mutual discussion. 'She talked to her aunt Bertram – she must talk to somebody of the ball, but her aunt had seen so little of what passed, and had so little curiosity, that it was heavy work. Lady Bertram was not certain of any body's dress, or any body's place at supper, but her own. "She could not recollect what it was that she had heard about one of the Miss Maddoxes, or what it was that Lady Prescott had noticed in Fanny; she was not sure whether Colonel Harrison had been talking of Mr Crawford or of William, when he said he was the finest young man in the room; somebody had whispered something to her; she had forgot to ask Sir Thomas what it could be". And

> '**How soon it is at an end! I wish it could all come over again!**'
> *The Watsons*

these were her longest speeches and clearest communications: the rest was only a languid "Yes, yes; very well; did you? did he? I did not see that – I should not know one from the other."' Fanny is forced to go to the parsonage for better conversation: 'the morning afforded her an opportunity of talking over Thursday night with Mrs Grant and Miss Crawford, in a very handsome style, with all the heightening of imagination and all the laughs of playfulness, which are so essential to the shade of a departed ball'. While it is hard to imagine 'laughs of playfulness' coming from Fanny herself, the satisfactory chat does succeed in bringing her mind 'into its everyday state' and calming her over-excited nerves.

Emma Watson can likewise share impressions of her ball with friends and family. She listens to Mr and Mrs Edwards discuss the assembly ball as soon as they get home, and the 'next morning brought a great many visitors. It was the way of the place always to call on Mrs Edwards on the morning after a ball', so Emma can spend all next morning 'discussing the merits of the ball with all this succession of company'. Tom Musgrave also pops in to talk it over and Emma then returns home to give her sister Elizabeth all the details. Elizabeth, who has regularly attended the D. balls for most of her life, is almost bursting for news: '"Now my dear Emma", said Miss Watson, as soon as they were alone, "you must talk to me all the rest of the day, without stopping, or I shall not be satisfied."'

Emma Woodhouse, however, never gets to talk over the Crown Inn ball with anyone. This novel illustrates a very different sort of after-effect following the dancing. Harriet Smith is left suffering from a cramp as a result of so much energetic movement, and this cramp immobilizes her when she is confronted by the gypsies. As the gypsies are more dangerous and exciting than a dance, they eclipse the ball in conversational importance. But Emma still manages to think over the night before, even if she cannot talk about it. Before Harriet's dramatic arrival she spends time walking about the Hartfield lawns and going over it all in her mind. And who does she think of first and most? Mr Knightley, of course!

The 'shade of a departed ball' adds greatly to the importance of the dance scenes in the novels. Post-mortems can emphasize the bonds of friendship and sisterhood, as well as reveal selfishness and vacuity of mind. They can reinforce a sense of community, transmit news and gossip, and provide an excuse for paying calls. The pleasure of a dance could be extended well and truly into all the next day.

Jane Austen talks over the ball

Jane Austen loved going to balls, but she gained almost equal pleasure from talking about them afterwards. If she had stayed the night with friends, then discussion was easy the next morning. When her closest confidante, sister Cassandra, was away, luckily for us, a letter replaced a chat. Jane Austen's correspondence reports on a delightful variety of dances. Her sharp eyes missed nothing, and she sent Cassandra witty summaries of local balls: 'Of the Gentlemen present You may have some idea from a list of my Partners. Mr Wood, G. Lefroy, Rice, a Mr Butcher . . . Mr Temple (not the horrid one of all), Mr Wm Orde . . . Mr John Harwood & Mr Calland, who appeared as usual with his hat in his hand, & stood every now and then behind Catherine & me to be talked to &

abused for not dancing. – We teized him however into it at last; – I was very glad to see him again after so long a separation, & he was altogether rather the Genius & Flirt of the Evening.' Cassandra, reading such comments, must have felt that she was at the ball too. Jane informed Cassandra how many were present ('Our ball on Thursday was a very poor one, only eight couple and but twenty-three people in the room; but it was not the ball's fault, for we were deprived of two or three families by the sudden illness of Mr Wither'), and she told Cassandra her views on those attending (Mrs Blount 'appeared exactly as she did in September, with the same broad face, diamond bandeau, white shoes, pink husband, & fat neck'). Indeed, Jane Austen could write so much on the subject of balls that she feared she would tire her correspondents: 'Your desiring to hear from me on Sunday will perhaps bring on you a more particular account of the Ball [at Hurstbourne] than you may care for, because one is prone to think much more of such things the morning after they happen, than when time has entirely driven them out of one's recollection.'

In return Jane heard from her sister about the balls Cassandra had attended: 'Again I return to my Joy that you danced at Ashford, & that you supped with the Prince.' In 1801 she wrote to Cassandra to say, 'it gives us great pleasure to know that the Chilham Ball was so agreable and that you danced four dances with Mr Kemble. – Desirable however, as the latter circumstance was I cannot help wondering at its taking place.' If Cassandra was slow to ask for news of a ball, Jane was quick to hurry her up: 'Your silence on the subject of our Ball, makes me suppose your Curiosity too great for words. We were very well entertained, & could have staid longer but for the arrival of my List shoes to convey me home, & I did not like to keep them waiting in the Cold.' There was much mutual pleasure in the Austen girls' post-mortems of dances. List shoes, by the way, were made of 'list', a sturdy, coarse material used for the edges of carpets and other woven fabrics.

Jane Austen also expected her family to send news of their balls. 'I depend on hearing from James very soon; he promised me an account of the Ball, and by this time he must have collected his Ideas enough, after the fatigue of dancing, to give me one.' As nieces and nephews grew up,

Aunt Jane entertained them with a game of imaginary conversations between them 'supposing [they] were all grown up, the day after a ball'. As adults, they too sent her gossipy reports: 'We had a very full & agreable account of Mr Hammond's Ball, from Anna [her niece] last night . . . I should like to have seen Anna's looks and performance.' In Jane Austen's view everyone should enjoy a ball and make that enjoyment last as long as possible. 'Dear Mrs Digweed!', she wrote of a neighbour at Steventon, 'I cannot bear that she should not be foolishly happy after a Ball.'

When Mr Bennet danced with Miss Gardiner at a ball, the custom of the time dictated that next morning he should call upon her to politely inquire about her health. By the time the Bennets' daughters are attending balls, one generation later, this custom was dying out. Earlier in the Georgian period, it was customary to dance the entire evening with one man (Fanny Burney's *Evelina* shows this happening), so a man had only one partner who needed to be visited the next day.

When Jane Austen danced with Tom Lefroy at Manydown, he visited the next day to see how she was. However, it is not common in Jane Austen's novels to see Darcy or Wickham, Henry Tilney or Edmund Bertram rushing off the following morning to see the women they had partnered the night before. Willoughby calls on Marianne, but as he does that every day regardless of what has taken place the night before, that can hardly be counted as a post-dance visit.

After the post-mortem, the dance was absolutely at an end. All that was left were the memories – of candle-lit rooms, of handsome men, of whispers and smiles, of feet moving gracefully in time with enchanting music, of pretty dresses or eye-catching scarlet coats, and of the promise of romance and dreams come true. And there was always the next ball to await eagerly, as Jane Austen and her characters so well appreciated: there is, quite simply, 'nothing like dancing after all'.

ance in Jane Austen films

'Every Hottentot can dance.'
Film script of the 1940 *Pride and Prejudice*

One of the great pleasures of watching a film adaptation of a Jane Austen novel is seeing beautifully dressed actors step out in handsome rooms to dance to lovely music. It is, however, a big challenge for a film-maker to create such scenes. Actors unused to formal dancing must learn the steps within a few days; in some of the longer television versions as many as a dozen separate dances needed to be mastered. Spoken lines must fit into the movement and music, and a large group of dancing people must be filmed from different camera angles. This is usually done in a stately home or historic building where slippery surfaces (one film crew poured Coca-Cola over the floors to prevent mishaps), valuable ornaments and poor lighting can all cause technical problems. However, balls are generally such a picturesque part of an adaptation that some scriptwriters add extra dances, which do not exist in the novel. In the BBC 1996 *Emma*, a harvest supper combined with a ball becomes the 'grand finale' of the film, drawing together all the cast in dancing harmony; while in Emma Thompson's 1995 film of *Sense and Sensibility* Willoughby snubs Marianne at a London ball instead of at the evening party described in the book.

Film-makers often choose a particular dance for its cinematic quality rather than its historical accuracy. In the 1940 *Pride and Prejudice* movie with Greer Garson and Laurence Olivier the costumes were better suited to *Gone with the Wind*; the dances performed in these crinolines were similarly inaccurate. Darcy and Elizabeth waltz together and even talk of it as a 'very modern' dance (in 1813 the waltz had yet to be introduced in England). Before their waltz Darcy utters one of the most absurd lines of the film, 'Every Hottentot can dance.'

The more stately spatial patterns of the dances enjoyed before Jane Austen was born have proven irresistible to film-makers. One example is 'Mr Beveridge's Maggot', a dance that dates back to 1695, quite likely a dance she'd never heard of. Yet it appears in the Netherfield ball scenes of the 1995 BBC *Pride and Prejudice* and again in the 1996 Gwyneth Paltrow film version of *Emma*. The BBC *Emma* includes 'Mr Isaac's Maggot' in its dance repertoire. A 'maggot' was an 'idea' or 'fancy' (as in the phrase 'to have a maggot in your brain') and Mr Beveridge and Mr Isaac would have been the dancing masters who first created those dances. In the 2007 television version of *Mansfield Park*, starring Billie Piper as Fanny Price, the characters dance on the lawn in mid-afternoon – outdoor dancing! Mr Woodhouse would have had a fit!

Anachronistic they might be, but there is no doubt that many directors have shown extensive skill in their depiction of dance scenes, using movement to convey a great deal of unspoken information to the viewer. No television audience needs to be verbally told that Mr Collins is a fool when they can see him on screen moving ineptly at every turn and treading on his partner's toes. Marianne's passion for Willoughby can be communicated without a word uttered if she is shown dancing joyfully with him, while Lydia Bennet's wildly enthusiastic style of dancing tells viewers all they need to know about the lack of restraint and the impropriety of her character. Personality, manners, rank, ambition and desire can all be revealed through dance by a talented director and crew.

It is hard to resist a ball scene when making a movie. Other Jane Austen films have been quick to provide their actors with a chance to dance on screen. *Becoming Jane* depicts Jane Austen at a ball, then roaming outside on the lawn in the dark with Tom Lefroy, and being kissed by him there. *Miss Austen Regrets* contains the inevitable country dance sequence; *Bride and Prejudice* includes a wonderful 'cobra dance'; *Clueless* has Cher and her LA friends dancing at someone's home (private ball) and at a frat party (assembly ball); and even the modern *The Jane Austen*

Book Club ends with a dinner dance. It is safe to say that so long as film-makers put Jane Austen's life and novels on screen, there will be delightful balls to watch and enjoy.

ᵐ

The most popular Jane Austen adaptation of all time is the BBC 1995 *Pride and Prejudice*, starring Colin Firth and Jennifer Ehle. The dances included are: 'The Touchstone' (1780), 'A Trip to Highgate' (1777), 'Mutual Love' (1777), 'The Comical Fellow' (1776), 'The Happy Captive' (1777), 'Pleasures of the Town' (1777), 'Barley Mow' (1779), 'Shrewsbury Lasses' (1765), 'Mr Beveridge's Maggot' (1695), 'Grimstock' (1651) and 'Lasses of Portsmouth' (1776). Jane Gibson, who was in charge of the dances, recalls in *The Making of Pride and Prejudice*: 'We had only three days to film the ball. We were using this large mansion and it was costing us a fortune; the money started ticking away the moment we arrived. It was such a complicated scene, I can remember the feeling of stark terror that we were going to fall behind. I saw a hundred people, all beautifully done up in costume and make-up . . . and they were all staring at me, waiting for instructions. Fortunately, we had planned it meticulously and we knew exactly the shots we were after.'

Bibliography

A Lady of Distinction, *Regency Etiquette: The Mirror of the Graces*, R.L. Shep, London, 1811.

Aldrich, Elizabeth, *From the Ballroom to Hell: Grace and Folly in Nineteenth-Century Dance*, Northwestern University Press, Evanston, Illinois, 1991.

Anstey, Christopher, *The New Bath Guide, Broadcast Books*, Bath, 1766.

Austen, Caroline, *Reminiscences*, ed. Deirdre Le Faye, Jane Austen Society, Winchester, 1986.

Austen, Jane, *Jane Austen's Letters*, ed. Deirdre Le Faye, Oxford University Press, Oxford, 1997.

Austen, Jane, *Selected Letters*, ed. Vivien Jones, Oxford University Press, Oxford, 2004.

Austen, Jane, *The Novels of Jane Austen*, Cambridge University Press, Cambridge: *Mansfield Park*, 2005; *Emma*, 2005; *Northanger Abbey* 2006; *Sense and Sensibility*, 2006; *Pride and Prejudice*, 2006; *Persuasion*, 2006; *Juvenilia*, 2006; *Later Manuscripts*, 2008.

Austen-Leigh, James Edward, *A Memoir of Jane Austen*, Folio Society, London, 1871.

Austen-Leigh, W.A., R.A. Austen-Leigh, and Deirdre Le Faye, *Jane Austen: A Family Record*, The British Library, London, 1989.

Birtwistle, Sue, and Susie Conklin, *The Making of Pride and Prejudice*, Penguin, London, 1995.

Birtwistle, Sue, and Susie Conklin, *The Making of Jane Austen's Emma*, Penguin, London, 1996.

Bradney-Smith, Adrienne, 'Music and Dance in the Time of Lady Susan and The Watsons', *JASA Chronicle*, The Jane Austen Society of Australia, Sydney, December 2010.

Brander, Michael, *The Georgian Gentleman*, Saxon House, Farnborough, 1973.

Byrde, Penelope, *Jane Austen Fashion: Fashion and Needlework in the Works of Jane Austen*, Excellent Press, Ludlow, 1999.

Cecil, David, *A Portrait of Jane Austen*, Constable, London, 1978.

Day, Malcolm, *Voices from the World of Jane Austen*, David & Charles, Cincinnati, 2006.

Downing, Sarah-Jane, *Fashion in the Time of Jane Austen*, Shire Publications, Oxford, 2010.

Dukes, Nicholas, *A Concise & Easy Method of Learning the Figuring Part of Country Dances. To Which is Prefixed the Figure of the Minuet*, N. Dukes, London, 1752.

Durang, Charles, *The Fashionable Dancer's Casket or the Ball-Room Instructor. A New and Splendid Work on Dancing, Etiquette, Deportment, and the Toilet*, Applewood Books, Bedford, 1856.

Elliott, Kirsten, *A Window on Bath*, Millstream Books, Bath, 1994.

Englehardt, Molly, 'The Manner of Reading: Jane Austen and the Semiotics of Dance', *Persuasions* No. 26, The Jane Austen Society of North America, 2004.

Fawcett, Trevor, *Bath Entertain'd: Amusements, Recreations and Gambling at the 18th-Century Spa*, Ruton, Bath, 1998.

Franks, A.H., *Social Dance: A Short History*, Routledge and Kegan Paul, London, 1963.

Gallini, Giovanni-Andrea, *Critical Observations on the Art of Dancing*, Gale, London, 1770.

Gisborne, Thomas, *Enquiry into the Duties of the Female Sex*, T. Cadell and W. Davies, London, 1797.

Gronow, Captain R.H., *Captain Gronow: His Reminiscences of Regency and Victorian Life, 1810–1860*, Kyle Cathie, London, 1862.

Hill, Constance, *Jane Austen: Her Homes and Her Friends*, Routledge, London, 1995.

Hinde, Thomas, *Tales from the Pump Room: Nine Hundred Years of Bath: The Place, the People and Its Gossip*, Victor Gollancz, London, 1988.

Jones, Hazel, *Jane Austen and Marriage*, Continuum, London, 2009.

Keller, Kate Van Winkle, and Genevieve Shimer, *The Playford Ball: 103 Early English Country Dances*, A Cappella Books and Country Dance and Song Society, Chicago, 1990.

Kloester, Jennifer, *Georgette Heyer's Regency World*, William Heinemann, London, 2005.

Jenyns, Soame, *The Art of Dancing, a Poem, in Three Canto's*, London, 1729.

Lane, Maggie, *Jane Austen's World: The Life and Times of England's Most Popular Author*, Carlton Press, London, 1996.

Lane, Maggie, *Jane Austen and Food*, Hambledon, London, 1995.

Laski, Marghanita, *Jane Austen and Her World*, Thames and Hudson, London, 1975.

Laudermilk, Sharon, and Teresa Hamlin, *The Regency Companion*, Garland Publishing, New York, 1989.

Le Faye, Deirdre, *Jane Austen: The World of Her Novels*, Frances Lincoln, London, 2002.

Lee-Riffe, Nancy, 'The Role of Country Dance in the Fiction of Jane Austen', *Women's Writing 5*, Routledge, London, 1998.

Low, Donald A., *That Sunny Dome: A Portrait of Regency Britain*, J.M. Dent & Sons, London, 1977.

Mansell, Darrell, *The Novels of Jane Austen: An Interpretation*, Macmillan, London, 1973.

McClure, Veronica Ann, 'English Country Dancing Before, During, and After Jane Austen', *Dixie Round Dance Council Newsletter*, Sharpsburg, Georgia, 2010.

Mingay, G.E., *Georgian London*, B.T. Batsford, London, 1975.

Mitton, G.E., *Jane Austen and Her Times*, Methuen & Co., London, 1905.

Murray, Venetia, *High Society: A Social History of the Regency Period 1788–1830*, Viking, London, 1998.

Parrill, Sue, *Jane Austen on Film and Television: A Critical Study of the Adaptations*, McFarland & Co., Jefferson, North Carolina, 2002.

Plumb, J.H., *Georgian Delights*, Weidenfeld & Nicolson, London, 1980.

Quirey, Belinda, *May I Have the Pleasure?: The Story of Popular Dancing*, Dance Books, Alton, Hampshire, 1987.

Reid-Walsh, Jacqueline, 'Entering the World of Regency Society: The Ballroom Scenes in *Northanger Abbey, The Watsons*, and *Mansfield Park*', *Persuasions* No. 16, The Jane Austen Society of North America, 1993.

Ross, Josephine, *Jane Austen: A Companion*, John Murray, London, 2002.

Selwyn, David, *Jane Austen and Leisure*, Hambledon, London, 1999.

Smollett, Tobias, *The Expedition of Humphry Clinker*, Penguin, London, 1771.

Spence, Jon, *Becoming Jane Austen*, Hambledon, London, 2003.

Thompson, Allison, *Dancing Through Time: Western Social Dance in Literature, 1400–1918*, McFarland & Co., Jefferson, North Carolina, 1998.

Thompson, Allison, 'The Felicities of Rapid Motion: Jane Austen in the Ballroom', *Persuasions* On-Line Vol. 21, Jane Austen Society of North America, 2000.

Tomalin, Claire, *Jane Austen: A Life*, Viking, London, 1997.

Tucker, George Holbert, *Jane Austen the Woman: Some Biographical Insights*, Robert Hale, London, 1994.

Vickery, Amanda, *The Gentleman's Daughter: Women's Lives in Georgian England*, Yale University Press, New Haven, 1998.

Watkins, Susan, *Jane Austen's Town and Country Style*, Rizzoli, New York, 1990.

Wilson, Cheryl, A., 'Dance, Physicality, and Social Mobility in Jane Austen's *Persuasion*', *Persuasions* No. 25, Jane Austen Society of North America, 2003.

Wilson, Cheryl A., *Literature and Dance in Nineteenth-Century Britain: Jane Austen to the New Woman*, Cambridge University Press, New York, 2009.

Wilson, Thomas, *An Analysis of Country Dancing*, W. Calvert, London, 1808.

Wilson, Thomas, *The Treasures of Terpsichore: or, A Companion for the Ball-Room*, Sherwood, Neely, and Jones, London, 1809.

Wilson, Thomas, *A Description of the Correct Method of Waltzing*, Sherwood, Neely, and Jones, London, 1816.

Wood, Melusine, *Historical Dances, 12th to 19th Century*, Dance Books, Alton, Hampshire, 1952.

Websites

kickery.com

earthlydelights.com.au/history

georgianindex.net/Dance/dance

A note about the text

All quotes in this book have been taken from the Cambridge University Press editions of Jane Austen's novels, minor works and juvenilia. These volumes were published between 2005 and 2008, each edited by a different Jane Austen scholar. They are authoritative and excellent editions.

Jane Austen's Letters, collected and edited by Deirdre Le Faye, and published by Oxford University Press in 1995, is the source for excerpts of her correspondence. This edition preserves Jane Austen's own spelling, capitalization and punctuation, as well as her frequent use of dashes.

Acknowledgments

The Jane Austen Society of Australia is the most wonderful literary society in the world and I am proud to be its president. This book is for all its members, in thanks for the friendship, encouragement, enthusiasm and support I have had for so many years. I hope every member enjoys reading it and that it makes them all return with increased pleasure to the novels of Jane Austen.

I would like to especially thank Helen Malcher for her invaluable assistance with illustrations and Julia Ermert for sending me so much helpful information on Regency dance, and for reading the manuscript. I wish I could personally thank Jon Spence, who tragically died while this book was being written. I will always treasure the memory of his friendship and our conversations about Jane Austen. I will miss his wit, his insights and the fun we had together.

Joan Strasbaugh of Jones Books came up with the original idea for this book and has been a fabulous editor and a pleasure to work with. I am extremely grateful to Jane Austen scholar Deirdre Le Faye for writing the foreword. Her superb edition of *Jane Austen's Letters* is a book that no one writing about Jane Austen can be without.

I come from a line of women who have loved reading Jane Austen. Sadly my mother is no longer here to read this book, but not a page of it was written without my thinking of her. I am so grateful to all my family – my wonderful children, Kenneth, Carrick, and Elinor, my husband Ian, my dad and my siblings. Thanks to you all.

Picture credits

Index